MY **FUNCTIONAL** SKILLS

MY **FUNCTIONA**

Level 1
English
Revision and Exam Practice

Victoria Eckert

HODDER Education

Photo credits: page 15 (left) © Fizkes/stock.adobe.com; page 15 (right) © Delcio Fernandes/peopleimages.com/stock.adobe.com; page 18 © Seventyfour/stock.adobe.com; page 27 © Gudellaphoto/stock.adobe.com; page 30 © Gstockstudio/stock.adobe.com; page 31 © Alexalmighty/stock.adobe.com; page 48 (top right) © Vitaliymateha/stock.adobe.com; page 48 (top left) © Zamrznuti tonovi/stock.adobe.com; page 48 (top centre) © C.Castilla/stock.adobe.com; page 48 (bottom centre) © Gorodenkoff/stock.adobe.com; page 48 (bottom left) © Adomo/stock.adobe.com; page 48 (bottom right) © Eileen/stock.adobe.com; page 58 © Abriendomundo/stock.adobe.com; page 59 (top) © Chris/stock.adobe.com; page 59 (bottom left) © Martin Siepmann/ImageBROKER/Alamy Stock Photo; page 59 (bottom centre) © Sergi Reboredo/Alamy Stock Photo; page 59 (bottom right) © Joshua P Jacks/Wirestock Creators/stock.adobe.com; page 60 (top right) © Eileen/stock.adobe.com; page 60 (bottom left) © Gemenacom/stock.adobe.com; page 60 (bottom right) © Andrey Solovev/stock.adobe.com; page 93 © Jonathan Nelson/Alamy Stock Photo

Every effort has been mad e to trace all copyright holders, but if any have been inadvertently overlooked, the Publishers will be pleased to make the necessary arrangements at the first opportunity.

Although every effort has been made to ensure that website addresses are correct at time of going to press, Hodder Education cannot be held responsible for the content of any website mentioned in this book. It is sometimes possible to find a relocated web page by typing in the address of the home page for a website in the URL window of your browser.

Hachette UK's policy is to use papers that are natural, renewable and recyclable products and made from wood grown in well-managed forests and other controlled sources. The logging and manufacturing processes are expected to conform to the environmental regulations of the country of origin.

Orders: please contact Hachette UK Distribution, Hely Hutchinson Centre, Milton Road, Didcot, Oxfordshire, OX11 7HH. Telephone: +44 (0)1235 827827. Email education@hachette.co.uk Lines are open from 9 a.m. to 5 p.m., Monday to Friday. You can also order through our website: www.hoddereducation.co.uk

ISBN: 9781398386983

© Victoria Eckert 2023

First published in 2023 by
Hodder Education,
An Hachette UK Company
Carmelite House
50 Victoria Embankment
London EC4Y 0DZ

www.hoddereducation.co.uk

Impression number   10 9 8 7 6 5 4 3 2 1

Year   2027 2026 2025 2024 2023

All rights reserved. Apart from any use permitted under UK copyright law, no part of this publication may be reproduced or transmitted in any form or by any means, electronic or mechanical, including photocopying and recording, or held within any information storage and retrieval system, without permission in writing from the publisher or under licence from the Copyright Licensing Agency Limited. Further details of such licences (for reprographic reproduction) may be obtained from the Copyright Licensing Agency Limited, www.cla.co.uk

Cover photo © danijelala - stock.adobe.com

Illustrations by Barking Dog Art

Typeset by Integra Software Services Pvt. Ltd., Pondicherry, India

Printed in Spain

A catalogue record for this title is available from the British Library.

Get the most from this book

We all need to decide how to revise in a way that works for us, but learning each topic, testing our understanding and knowing how to answer exam questions is essential.

My Functional Skills will help you to do that in a planned way, topic by topic. Use this book in the way that works best for you: write in it, doodle, personalise your notes, and check your progress by ticking off each section as you revise.

Features to help you succeed

DIAGNOSTIC QUESTIONS

Focus! Work out which topics you need to spend more time on by answering these **diagnostic questions**. You can choose to focus on areas where you're weaker and spend less time on the topics you're already really good at.

WORKED EXAMPLE

Oh, so that's how I do it! Every topic includes at least one **worked example** that guides you through the steps to answer an exam-style question.

KEY TERMS

What does that mean? On each page all the important key terms are defined, and there's a handy summary of all of these in the glossary at the back of the book.

EXAM TIP

What is the examiner looking for? Throughout the book you'll find **hints and tips** on how to approach answering questions, as well as how you might gain the most marks in the exam.

COMMON MISTAKES

Where did I go wrong? Many of the **common mistakes** and pitfalls students have made in Functional Skills exams are highlighted, so you can avoid making them yourself.

CHECK YOUR UNDERSTANDING

Now it's my turn! Test your understanding of each topic with these short questions.

EXAM-STYLE QUESTIONS

Practice, practice, practice! Get exam ready by answering these **exam-style questions**. Review the **answers** online at www.hoddereducation.co.uk/functional-skills-english-answers to see whether you have answered correctly or where you went wrong.

My revision planner

Use this revision planner to plan your revision, topic by topic. Tick each box when you have:
- revised and understood a topic
- tested yourself
- practised exam questions and gone online to check your answers.

       Countdown to my exams   6

       Assessment breakdown   7

1 Speaking, listening and communicating

1.1 Identify relevant information and lines of argument in explanations or presentations   12

1.2 Make requests and ask relevant questions to obtain specific information in different contexts   14

1.3 Respond effectively to detailed questions   15

1.4 Communicate information, ideas and opinions clearly and accurately on a range of topics   17

1.5 Express opinions and arguments and support them with evidence   20

1.6 Follow and understand discussions and make contributions relevant to the situation and the subject   21

1.7 Use appropriate phrases and registers, and adapt contributions to take account of audience, purpose and medium   23

1.8 Respect the turn-taking rights of others during discussions, using appropriate language for interjection   25

2 Reading

2.1 Identify and understand the main points, ideas and details in texts   33

2.2 Compare information, ideas and opinions in different texts   35

2.3 Identify meanings in texts and distinguish between fact and opinion   38

2.4 Recognise that language and other textual features can be varied to suit different audiences and purposes   41

2.5 Use reference materials and appropriate strategies (e.g. using knowledge of different word types) for a range of purposes, including to find the meaning of words   43

2.6 Understand organisational and structural features and use them to locate relevant information (e.g. index, menus, subheadings, paragraphs) in a range of straightforward texts   45

2.7	Infer from images meanings not explicit in the accompanying text	48
2.8	Recognise vocabulary typically associated with specific types and purposes of texts (e.g. formal, informal, instructional, descriptive, explanatory and persuasive)	51
2.9	Read and understand a range of specialist words in context	54
2.10	Use knowledge of punctuation to aid understanding of straightforward texts	56

3 Writing

3.1	Use a range of punctuation correctly (e.g. full stops, question marks, exclamation marks, commas, possessive apostrophes)	67
3.2	Use correct grammar (e.g. subject–verb agreement, consistent use of different tenses, definite and indefinite articles)	71
3.3	Spell words used most often in work, study and daily life, including specialist words	74
3.4	Communicate information, ideas and opinions clearly, coherently and accurately	76
3.5	Write text of an appropriate level of detail and of appropriate length (including where this is specified) to meet the needs of purpose and audience	79
3.6	Use format, structure and language appropriate for audience and purpose	81
3.7	Write consistently and accurately in complex sentences, using paragraphs where appropriate	89
	Language techniques, layout features and purposes of texts	99
	Glossary	100
	Answers to diagnostic questions	102
	Index	110

Countdown to my exams

6–8 WEEKS TO GO

- **What do I need to revise?** Familiarise yourself with the topics you need to revise. You can use the Revision Planner in this book to help you.
- **What will the exam look like?** Look at the exam board specification or ask your tutor about the format of your Functional Skills exams: when and where will they take place? How long will they last? What types of questions might I see on the exam papers? The assessment breakdown on page 7 gives more information on this.
- **Get organised.** Organise your notes and make sure you've covered all the topics.
- **Make a plan.** Create a revision plan that shows the days and times you'll revise each topic. Be realistic – small, focused sessions of around 40–50 minutes will be more achievable and successful. Make sure you allow yourself breaks. Stick to your plan!

2–6 WEEKS TO GO

- **Make a start.** Use your own revision plan to work through the topics in this book. Look at the explanations, worked examples, key terms, common mistakes and hints and tips. Highlight any important bits and make your own notes in the book if you wish. Tick off each topic when you feel confident, or come back to any topics you think you need to look at again.
- **What do I know?** Now test your understanding by answering the Check Your Understanding questions. Look at the answers online at www.hoddereducation.co.uk/functional-skills-english-answers. What did you get right? Which topics do you need to revisit?
- **Where do I need help?** Speak to your tutor about any topics you're finding tricky. They may be able to go over them again with you as part of a revision class.
- **Get exam ready!** The best way to prepare is to practise answering lots and lots of exam questions. Have a go at the Exam-style Questions in this book and check your answers online at www.hoddereducation.co.uk/functional-skills-english-answers. Look at and attempt past Functional Skills exam papers – you will find these on your exam board's website, or your tutor will be able to share some with you.
- **Keep track.** Use the Revision Planner to keep track of your progress.

1 WEEK TO GO

- **Have I covered everything?** Check that you have revised every topic on the Revision Planner. Look at any you haven't already now, and revisit any topics you still feel less confident about.
- **Prepare for exam conditions.** Do a complete past exam paper in timed exam conditions to help you plan your time for the real exams. Compare your answers against the mark scheme or ask your tutor to mark it for you.

THE DAY BEFORE

- **Last-minute check.** Read through your notes and flick through this book to remind yourself of any important points, common mistakes and hints and tips.
- **When and where is it?** Check the time and place of your exam and plan your journey, allowing plenty of time to make sure you're there on time.
- **What do I need to take?** Make sure you have everything you need for the exam – pens, highlighters and water.
- **Relax!** Your revision is complete. Give yourself some time to relax and get an early night to make sure you're ready for the exam tomorrow.

MY FUNCTIONAL SKILLS EXAMS

Speaking, listening and communicating exam

Date:

Time:

Location:

Reading exam

Date:

Time:

Location:

Writing exam

Date:

Time:

Location:

Assessment breakdown

The Functional Skills English exams will test you on three different elements of English that are used in **work, study and life**:
- Speaking, listening and communicating
- Reading
- Writing

Your speaking, listening and communicating exam

The speaking, listening and communicating exam may take place in your usual classroom or learning environment. It will not involve sitting quietly and writing answers; instead, you will be taking part in group activities that involve talking and listening to others. It might feel less formal than a sit-down exam, but you should still take it seriously.

There are **three activities** in this exam:

1. You will give your own talk or presentation on a familiar topic, chosen by you (lasting about 3–8 minutes). This will be followed by a question-and-answer session or informal discussion, in which you will answer questions about your presentation.

2. You will take part in a question-and-answer session or informal discussion (lasting about 5–10 minutes) following someone else's presentation. This might be recorded or given by one of your fellow students. You will need to ask **at least one question** about the presentation you have just heard.

3. You will take part in a group discussion (lasting about 10–12 minutes) on a topic given to you beforehand, not chosen by you. This topic will most likely be **unfamiliar**, meaning you will need to research it to gain more information, ideas and opinions.

Preparation time

You will be given preparation time before the exam, usually at least one week. This should be used for **researching and preparing your presentation**, including any slides or handouts you choose to use. You should not write a full script to read from – you will not be allowed to do this.

You should also **research the discussion topic** and plan what you would like to talk about. You can write notes that list key details, but you **cannot** write a script.

Your reading exam

You will be given **two or three source documents** to read. These will be linked by the same or a similar topic. They could be articles, adverts, leaflets, webpages, blog posts, emails, letters or many other kinds of document.

You will be asked questions about these source documents, which will test the skills described in the reading learning objectives in this book.

The questions might be asked in different ways:
- Some questions will ask you to choose one or more correct answers from a list of options (known as multiple choice questions). Make sure you read the question carefully so you know how many answers to tick.
- Some questions will ask you to find information, details or ideas in the source documents. You can often answer these with **quotes/quotations** from the text, or you may find it easier to explain what the text says in your own words.
- Some questions will ask for quotations. You should answer these with the **exact words** used in the document.

You are not always expected to write in full sentences, and sometimes a one-word answer is enough. Sometimes, however, you will need to answer with more detail. Read the question carefully to see if your response **fully** answers it. For example:

What is one product sold in Holly's shop?

✓ Milk
  This is enough to answer the question fully.

✓ One product sold in Holly's shop is milk.
  While this is a correct answer, you do not need to write a full sentence or repeat the question. This will just waste time.

Explain why Holly is having trouble making enough money from her shop.

✗ Bread
  There is not enough information here to answer the question.

✓ People are not buying as much bread as they used to.
  This goes into enough detail to answer the question.

> ✓ A green tick means this is a good answer.
> ✓ A yellow tick means this answer may be acceptable, but it could be worded better or expanded upon.
> ✗ A red X means this answer is not correct.

There may be other kinds of questions, such as ones that ask you to tick boxes to show if something is true or false, if it is fact or opinion, or which document the information comes from.

If you come across an unexpected style of question, don't panic. Just read the instructions in the question **carefully** so you understand what you are expected to do.

Important information about the exam

- You are allowed to use a dictionary.
- There will be a total of **25–30 marks** available across **15–20 questions**.
- The marks available for each question will be shown in brackets.
- You will be given **two or three source documents**. These could be in a separate booklet or included in the question booklet. They might be referred to as documents, texts or sources.
- Make sure you **read instructions carefully** so you know which source document to use for each question.

Your writing exam

The writing paper has **two questions**. Both will test you on the writing learning objectives explained in this book.

Each question includes some important information, followed by a task. You must read **all** of this very carefully – **do not** skip straight to the task.

The information and task will tell you:

- What **text type** you should write, such as a letter, email, report, narrative, etc. For more information on these, see **section 3.6** on page 81.
- **Who** you are writing to or for. If you are writing a letter or email, you should be given the postal address or email address to write to.
- **Why** you are writing, such as to persuade, to apply, to complain, etc.
- Any **specific details** that you **need** to include. Do not ignore these.
- **Extra information** to help with the task. This will usually be included above the task and it is very important to pay attention to it. For example, if you are asked to write a complaint, the extra information might tell you more about the problem you encountered.
- **How long** your answer should be. This might be a word count, a rough number of paragraphs to aim for, or a recommended amount of time to spend on your answer.

You should answer **both** writing questions. If you are running out of time, write down what you can, even in a rough or bullet-point form. Remember, any answer is better than no answer.

Leave yourself some time to check your writing at the end of the exam. You are bound to find some mistakes that you can fix, which could mean the difference between a pass and a fail.

Important information about the exam

- You are **not allowed** a dictionary or any other spelling or grammar aid.
- The total marks available can vary with different papers, from 27 to 54 marks. You can check this with your tutor or teacher beforehand.
- There are **two questions**.
- The marks for each question are shown in brackets.
- You will be assessed on spelling, punctuation and grammar in **both** tasks.

1 Speaking, listening and communicating

DIAGNOSTIC QUESTIONS

When you have answered the following questions, turn to pages 102 to 103 for the correct answers and explanations. You will also find advice and support here to help you identify the chapters you will need to focus on.

1   You are listening to a presentation about horse riding. The presenter mentions all the points below. Select which **three** you think are the **most** important pieces of information for you to remember.

   ☐ How long the presenter expects the presentation to take

   ☐ What riding a horse involves

   ☐ The equipment needed to ride and look after horses

   ☐ A joke about horses

   ☐ What the presenter had for breakfast on her first day of horse riding

   ☐ The presenter's opinion about horse riding

2   The presentation about horse riding has finished and it is time for questions.

   Which **two** questions in the list below would be the **best** ones to ask?

   a   What is a good name for a horse?
   b   Do horses really eat carrots?
   c   What kinds of horses are the best to ride and why?
   d   How expensive is horse riding as a regular hobby?
   e   What is your favourite film about horses?

3   It is time for you to give your own presentation.

   Number the following stages of your presentation so they are in the correct logical order.

Stage	Number
Give your own point of view.	☐
Present information and ideas.	☐
Ask if the audience has any questions.	☐
Introduce the topic.	☐

4 You are talking about why dogs make great pets. Select which **three** pieces of evidence you think would be the **best** to back up your opinion with.

☐ A personal story about your dog providing comfort when you are sad

☐ The name of a celebrity's dog

☐ Your own opinion that dogs are amazing

☐ The fact that a third of all households around the world have a dog

☐ The fact that dogs evolved from wolves

☐ Explaining the games you can play with a dog and the tricks you can teach it

5 What is the most appropriate response to each situation? Choose a or b for each situation.

Situation	Response
During an informal question-and-answer session, another student asks what you think is the best holiday.	a 'Wow, that's a tough question! I think I'd have to go with beach holidays because I love lying in the sun, and I also love water sports.' b 'It is a complicated issue. You need to weigh up the good and bad points of each holiday before you make a decision.'
Someone has just finished their presentation about how they achieved their goal to climb England's highest mountain. You have also climbed that mountain several times.	a 'Oh, anyone can climb a mountain. I've climbed all the mountains in the Lake District and that includes England's highest mountain.' b 'Congratulations on your achievement! I also love climbing mountains. Can you tell us a bit more about how you got into it?'
Everyone looks confused when you use a complicated word.	a Make sure you don't use that word again. b Explain clearly what the word means.

1 Speaking, listening and communicating

1.1 Identify relevant information and lines of argument in explanations or presentations

REVISED

In your exam, you will listen to a **presentation**, which might be recorded or might be given by one of your fellow students. You don't need to remember everything you hear, but you should **listen carefully** for:

- **Relevant information** – this means the **main subjects** as well as **important details** like names, dates, times, directions and instructions.
- **Lines of argument** – this means the **points** the speaker is making and any **opinions** they give. You should be able to understand the **reasons** for their opinions.

After the presentation, there will be a question-and-answer session or informal discussion – this is when you need to show that you have understood the speaker's points and that you have been able to pick out important information. You can show this by:

- asking questions to find out more information. For example:
  → *'How do you protect yourself from cold weather when you're riding your motorbike?'*
- asking for the speaker's opinion on something. For example:
  → *'Do you find riding the motorbike harder than cycling?'*
- saying whether you agree or disagree with one of the speaker's opinions. For example:
  → *'I agree that motorbikes look cool, but I don't think I would be brave enough to ride one.'*
- mentioning one of the points the speaker made. For example:
  → *'If you use so little fuel in a month, it definitely does sound cheaper than running a car.'*

> **Presentation**: preparing and then giving information out loud to an audience.
>
> **Relevant information**: what the presentation is about, including the main subjects and any information and facts that relate to these.
>
> **Lines of argument**: how the different points that someone makes lead to their opinions or conclusions.

COMMON MISTAKE

Try not to be too vague. Here is an example of what works and what does not:

✓ *'I will definitely be more aware of motorbikes when I'm on the roads now, especially after you told us how quiet electric motorbikes are.'*

This works because it mentions one of the speaker's points (electric motorbikes are quiet) and responds to one of the speaker's arguments (people need to be more aware of motorbikes). Your marker will know that you have listened and understood.

✗ *'I think we should all follow your advice.'*

This only shows general agreement rather than an understanding of the speaker's points.

1 Speaking, listening and communicating

EXAM TIP

It can be helpful to quickly note down important information while listening to a presentation. Then, when you contribute to the question-and-answer session or discussion afterwards, you can glance at your notes to help you remember these details.

Types of bike – cruiser, sports
Protective clothes – helmet, special jacket, boots
First ever motorbike 1885 top speed 12mph

WORKED EXAMPLE

Question-and-answer session

Read the transcript on page 27 of a short presentation about playing guitar. The following comments were part of a question-and-answer session after this presentation.

'Can you tell us why you use a pick instead of your fingers to pluck strings?'

'Why do you need to plug an electric guitar into an amplifier?'

✓ These comments show that the listeners have picked out and understood relevant details from the speech, in this case information about guitar picks and amplifiers.

'I agree that everyone remembers guitar players. Jimmy Hendrix, Eric Clapton, Jimmy Page … I can name so many. I'd love to learn to play guitar.'

'You said guitar is the most fun instrument to play, but I actually think drums are better. It's more energetic. But if you really want to be remembered, you need to be the singer.'

✓ These comments show that the listeners have understood the speaker's points. They have mentioned those points and have given their own opinions too.

CHECK YOUR UNDERSTANDING

Ask a friend, family member or colleague to tell you about their own special interest. Then complete the following tasks.

1   Write one sentence explaining what their special interest involves and why they enjoy it.

2   Write down three **details** about their special interest. This could be something about its history, an item or material they use while doing it, the name of a famous person with the same interest, the occasion they first became interested in it, or any other details.

3   Write down one of their opinions about this special interest. Give your own opinion as well.

1.2 Make requests and ask relevant questions to obtain specific information in different contexts

REVISED

In the question-and-answer session following someone else's presentation, as well as in the group discussion, you will need to ask questions to gain more information or to find out someone's opinion. You should ask **at least one question** in each.

Your questions should be:
- **clear and to the point**; otherwise, the person you are asking might not understand what it is you want to know
- **on the topic** that is being discussed (relevant questions).

> **Relevant questions**: questions that are about the topic being discussed.

EXAM TIP

It is better to ask questions that are as **open** as possible. This means your question should encourage a detailed response rather than a simple yes or no answer. For example:

✓ 'What are some of the traits that make Labradors good family pets?'

✓ 'Are Labradors good family pets?'
This question is not as useful as the question above because it can be answered with just a yes or no.

WORKED EXAMPLE

Question-and-answer session

Read the transcript on page 27 of a short presentation about playing guitar. The following question was asked after this presentation.

'Can you explain more about the differences between acoustic and classical guitars?'

✓ This is a good question. It is easy to understand what is being asked. It is on the topic of guitars, which is what the presentation was about. It invites a detailed answer – it cannot be answered with just a yes or no.

Group discussion

In the group discussion, the group are discussing the topic: **should more people take holidays in the UK rather than travel abroad?**

One of the group members says that holidays at home are more environmentally friendly. A different group member then asks:

'Why is it more environmentally friendly? Can you explain more about that?'

✓ This is another good question. It is clear and easy to understand. It is on the topic of holidays, and it responds to something that a group member has said. It invites a detailed answer that will help keep the discussion going.

CHECK YOUR UNDERSTANDING

Ask a friend, family member or colleague to tell you about a recent holiday. When they have finished talking, ask them questions to find out the following information:
1. More details about where they stayed, for example a hotel, a tent, a rental
2. Details about something that happened on their holiday
3. Whether they would recommend the holiday and why

1.3 Respond effectively to detailed questions

REVISED

You should be able to **answer clearly any questions** on your presentation topic, as well as questions asked during the group discussion. You need to listen to the question **carefully** so that you can answer effectively.

What if I don't know the answer?

Don't panic. If you don't know the answer, it is fine to say so, but try **not** to just say 'I don't know' and leave it there. Here are some things you could do instead:

- It is OK to say that you are not sure, but that you can make an educated guess. Then say what you think the answer is.
- Ask for more information. For example, you could say: *'Unfortunately, I'm not as familiar with that side of it. Is it something you could explain more about?'*
- Tell the person who asked the question that you will need to do more research and get back to them later. Remember to thank them for raising an interesting question that gives you more to think about.

> **Answer effectively:** answer in a way that gives enough information and fully answers the question.

COMMON MISTAKE

Do not groan, roll your eyes or look irritated by questions. Instead, you should look interested, smile and nod. Remember, questions show that people have listened to you and are interested in what you have to say, so try to show that you are happy to be asked.

EXAM TIP

When preparing for your presentation and for the group discussion, think about what questions you are likely to be asked. Make sure you have enough information to answer well. If you are prepared, you will be able to answer with more confidence.

1 Speaking, listening and communicating

> **WORKED EXAMPLE**
>
> **Question-and-answer session**
>
> Read the transcript on page 27 of a short presentation about playing guitar. After this presentation, the following questions were asked and answered.
>
> **Question:** *'Is the guitar hard to play?'*
>
> ✗ **Answer:** *'No.'*
>
> This is not a good answer. Although this question *can* be answered with just a yes or no, you should always try to give more information than this. Pretend the person asking the question added 'and why?' onto the end of their question. Explain your **reasons** for saying yes or no.
>
> **Question:** *'I want to start learning to play guitar. Can you tell me how I should begin?'*
>
> ✓ **Answer:** *'That's a great question, and I'm so excited you want to learn! The first step is to decide if you want to play electric or acoustic guitar. Borrow one from a friend or try different ones out in a music shop to see what you like. Once you have a guitar, you need to know how to hold it properly and learn what all the parts of it are called. There are some great tutorials online that you can watch. Just search for 'learn guitar for beginners'.*
>
> This clearly answers the question, including plenty of detail so that the questioner gets the information they want. The words 'That's a great question' show that the question is appreciated.

> **CHECK YOUR UNDERSTANDING**
>
> Give a short presentation to a friend, family member or colleague about one of your special interests. They should then ask you the following questions, and you should answer as effectively as you can.
>
> 1. Can you explain more about how you first became interested in this?
> 2. Can you tell me a fun fact about your special interest?
> 3. How could I find out more about your special interest and get involved in it myself?

1 Speaking, listening and communicating

1.4 Communicate information, ideas and opinions clearly and accurately on a range of topics

REVISED

In your presentation and in the group discussion, you should be able to **give clear information** about the topic you are talking about. This includes:

- going into more detail on important points
- explaining anything that is complicated
- explaining things that are new to your audience, even if you are very familiar with them yourself
- giving reasons for your opinions.

Before you give your presentation, you will have time to prepare. You should:

- make sure you know enough about your topic and what you want to say about it
- make sure you know how to give the information clearly and in a logical order
- decide if you want to use slides or images and prepare these if you do
- think about what questions you might be asked
- practise your presentation so you are confident when it's time to give it.

You are **NOT** allowed to write a full script for your presentation.

> A good presentation will follow this (or a similar) structure:
> 1 Introduce the topic.
> 2 Present information and ideas.
> 3 Give your own point of view.
> 4 Ask the audience for their point of view.

During your presentation, you should speak:

- clearly and confidently
- a little slower than normal so the audience can properly take in what you are saying
- with an interested voice – you don't want to bore your audience.

EXAM TIP

Bringing pre-prepared notes to your presentation can help you to remember **important points**. Only write down small pieces of information to use as reminders, such as a word or two for each point you want to cover.

> Intro: how I began netball
> rules of game
> my position – goal defence
> importance of team work
> why I love it
> ask if any audience members play

1 Speaking, listening and communicating

EXAM TIP

Think about your expressions and your body language:
- Whether you are standing or sitting, **do not** slump or look bored.
- Look at your audience throughout your presentation. **Do not** stare over their heads or at a spot on the wall.
- If you are using slides, **do not** turn your back on the audience to look at them.

COMMON MISTAKE

If you are using notes, **do not** look down at them all the time. They are only meant to be quick reminders that you glance at when needed.

WORKED EXAMPLE

Read the transcript on page 27 of a short presentation about playing guitar.

This presentation is mostly successful, but there are also things that could be better.

Good points	Things that could be better
✓ Greets everybody, then introduces the topic straight away.	
✓ Starts in a logical place – how she became interested in guitar.	
✓ Gives clear, detailed information about different kinds of guitar.	✗ Mentions but does not explain about classical guitars. ✗ Does not explain what an amplifier does. ✗ Does not explain the specialist word 'fret', which the audience are unlikely to be familiar with.
✓ Explains how guitars make sound and notes.	✗ Does not explain terms like 'pluck', 'strum' and 'chords'. This makes the explanation harder to understand.

1 Speaking, listening and communicating

Good points	Things that could be better
✓ Makes her opinions clear: *'guitars are amazing'*, *'undeniably cooler'*, *'it becomes part of your identity'*.	✗ Does not always explain *why* she think what she does. *'Obviously, being into rock and metal, I chose the electric guitar.'* The reason might not be obvious to the audience.
✓ Includes a picture of her pick. You do not need to include images or slides in your presentation, but it can add interest for the audience. Here, this is a nice personal touch.	✗ Still does not explain what a pick actually is.
✓ Gives good, detailed reasons why she loves playing guitar and why she would recommend it.	
✓ Finishes the presentation nicely by thanking the audience for listening, then asks if anyone has questions.	

CHECK YOUR UNDERSTANDING

Give a short presentation to a friend, family member or colleague about something you love. It could be your favourite food, favourite music, a sport you love, or anything else. When you have finished, ask them for feedback about the following things:

1 Did they understand everything you had to say? See if they can remember three important points from your presentation.

2 Do they know what your opinion on your topic is? If not, how could you have made this clearer?

3 What was good or bad about your tone of voice and body language? Did you speak at the right speed or were you a little too slow or fast?

1.5 Express opinions and arguments and support them with evidence

REVISED

During your presentation and in the group discussion, you should be able to explain your opinions and arguments, using evidence to back them up. This evidence could be:

- **Facts**. For example: *There are 5.25 trillion pieces of plastic in the oceans.*
- **Examples**. For example: *Rescuers saved Huzza the dolphin from the plastic she was trapped in.*
- **Quotes** from experts. For example: *Dr Know, a prominent scientist, said 'Plastic is a terrible threat to wildlife.'*
- **Your own or others' experience**. For example: *Every day I walk my dog along the beach and it is covered in plastic waste.*
- Any other points that **back up** your argument.

> **Evidence**: information that backs up arguments and opinions, such as facts, examples, experience, observations and quotes.

WORKED EXAMPLE

Read the transcript on page 27 of a short presentation about playing guitar.

Kelly uses different kinds of evidence to back up her opinions and arguments.

Argument / Opinion	Evidence
Guitars are amazing	✓ Personal experience – she tells us all about how she became interested in guitars.
	✓ Explanation of how a guitar makes sound and notes.
Picks can express your personality	✓ Image of her pick, which reflects Kelly's personality. You don't have to include images or slides in your presentation, but it can be effective as evidence.
Recommends the guitar	✓ Mentions that studies have shown playing guitar releases dopamine, the body's feel-good hormone.
	✓ Uses a fact – the guitar is the second most played instrument in the world after the piano.
The guitar becomes part of a guitarist's identity	✓ Gives a quote from a famous guitarist that backs this up – Joan Jett: *'My guitar is not a thing. It is an extension of myself. It is who I am.'*

> **EXAM TIP**
>
> It can be effective to repeat information that you want your audience to pay extra attention to. For example: *'Did you know that there are 5.25 trillion pieces of plastic in the oceans? Yes, that's right! 5.25 trillion!'*

> **COMMON MISTAKE**
>
> If you decide to use slides to help present evidence, make sure you don't overload each slide with too much information. This will be hard to follow and might cause the audience to read the slide rather than listen to you.

CHECK YOUR UNDERSTANDING

Prepare one piece of evidence to back up each of the following three statements. You are allowed to look online or anywhere else for evidence. Your evidence could be facts, examples, quotes, your own or others' experience, or anything else that supports the statement.

1. Climate change is real.
2. Too much sugar can be harmful to health.
3. It is important to get enough sleep.

1.6 Follow and understand discussions and make contributions relevant to the situation and the subject

REVISED

As part of your speaking, listening and communication exam, you will take part in a group discussion with other students. The topic will be given to you before the exam so that you can spend some time researching it. In this preparation time, you need to make sure you know enough about the topic to talk about it with others, and to form your own opinions about it.

During the group discussion, you need to make **contributions** (comments and questions) that are **relevant** (on topic). You could:

- give more information that has not been mentioned yet
- give more evidence to support an argument
- give your own opinion, or agree or disagree with someone else's opinion (try to always give reasons for your opinion as well)
- talk a little about your own experience with this topic
- ask questions to get more information or to understand something better
- ask questions to find out someone else's opinion.

> **Contribution**: a comment or question that adds something to the discussion.

You need to make sure that what you say fits into the conversation the group is having. For example, if they are talking about different sports they think colleges should offer students, it would not make sense to ask: *'Do you think it's more fun to score goals or to defend the goal?'* While this question is on the topic of sport, it does not fit into the conversation the other group members are having.

> **EXAM TIP**
>
> Involving others is a great way to keep the discussion going. For example, after giving your own opinion, you could invite others to talk by saying: *'Does anyone else have any thoughts about this?'*

> **COMMON MISTAKE**
>
> **Do not** interrupt people or talk over them. Do not make a dismissive or rude comment. These are not good contributions to a discussion.

WORKED EXAMPLE

Group discussion

The discussion topic is: **should colleges do more to help their students stay healthy?** The group is currently talking about whether colleges should offer classes that promote good mental health.

The following conversation takes place:

Tarone: 'I think classes on mindfulness could be really helpful for students.'

Amelia: 'That sounds interesting. What is mindfulness exactly?'

> ✓ Amelia asks a question to get more information. Her question is on topic and is a relevant response to what Tarone has just said.

Tarone: 'It's about paying more attention to what's happening right now, like the feel of your feet on the ground and anything you can smell or hear. It helps you feel calm and less stressed. It stops negative thoughts.'

> ✓ Tarone provides a clear and useful explanation. This adds to the discussion by giving the other group members more information about the topic.

Amelia: 'That's a good idea. Having the skills to focus your mind away from negative thoughts would help a lot of students.'

> ✓ Amelia does not stop at 'That's a good idea'. She adds more to the discussion by giving reasons for her opinion.

Emma: 'I think colleges should get rid of vending machines that sell sugary drinks and sweets.'

> ✓ Emma's comment is on the topic of how colleges can do more to help their students stay healthy.
>
> ✗ However, her comment does **not** fit into the current conversation because it is not about mental health. That means it is not relevant to the situation.

CHECK YOUR UNDERSTANDING

Look at Emma's last comment in the worked example above.
1. Which one of the following comments would have been a better contribution from Emma?
   a. Do you think colleges should do more to help their students stay healthy?
   b. I think a variety of options would help students most.
   c. But what is mindfulness?
   d. I don't get negative feelings. It's your own fault if you have them.
2. Tarone would like to change the subject. He has a lot to say about colleges offering sports to keep students physically healthy. What is the best way for him to start talking about this?
   a. I really love sports. I think colleges should offer all kinds of different sports to students.
   b. I'm sick of talking about mental health. Let's move on to physical health.
   c. What kinds of sports do you play, Emma? What about you, Amelia?
   d. Sports and exercise are also ways to encourage good mental health, and they're good for physical health too.
3. Amelia has a personal story about how playing sports helped her to manage her stress. Would it be appropriate for her to tell this story now? Why, or why not?

1 Speaking, listening and communicating

1.7 Use appropriate phrases and registers, and adapt contributions to take account of audience, purpose and medium

REVISED

This learning objective sounds complicated, but it just means that you need to use words and expressions (**phrases**) and a tone of voice (**register**) that suits the situation. You should:

- Use words and expressions that the people listening to you (your **audience**) can understand.
- **Adapt** (change) your words and expressions when the situation or **medium** changes. For example:
  - If you are giving a presentation on a fun and informal topic, you could use conversational language.
  - If you are in a serious or formal discussion, you should not use chatty language or tell jokes.
  - If you are explaining something, use clear, simple words and short sentences.
  - If your **purpose** is to try to get your listeners to agree with you, use persuasive language.
- Speak with an **appropriate** tone of voice for the situation you are in. For example:
  - If you are giving a presentation about something you enjoy, you should speak enthusiastically.
  - If you are talking about a serious topic, use a serious tone of voice.
  - **Never** use a dismissive or angry tone.
- Change the way you speak when needed. For example:
  - If you are making an important point, you might want to speak a little louder than normal.
  - If you are explaining something complicated, you may need to speak more slowly.

> **Phrases:** the words and expressions you use.
>
> **Registers:** the tone of voice you speak with.
>
> **Audience:** the people listening to you.
>
> **Adapt:** change to fit the current situation.
>
> **Medium:** the type of speaking you are doing, such as a presentation, a discussion, or a question-and-answer session.
>
> **Purpose:** what you are trying to achieve, such as to give information, to explain something or to convince someone.
>
> **Appropriate:** suitable.

EXAM TIP

Adapting in the group discussion is about **being aware of the other members of the group** and what they are talking about. You need to pay attention to what other people are saying, their tone of voice and the topic they are discussing. Make sure your comments fit into the conversation.

WORKED EXAMPLE

Group discussion

The discussion topic is: **should people do more to support charities?** The group is currently discussing fundraising events.

The following conversation takes place:

Tarone: 'Fundraising events are always more successful when they're fun. The word "fun" is even in the name.'

Emma: 'That's true. My friend once raised money for charity by sitting in a bath full of beans. People sponsored her to do it because it was such a funny idea. One person said they would donate double the amount if she included spaghetti hoops in the bath, so she did.'

> Emma uses a funny personal story that fits with the light-hearted subject matter.

Later, the discussion turns to the reasons charities need money.

Amelia: 'In the end, the money raised goes towards easing suffering, whether it's supporting people with illness, saving abused animals, giving disaster relief, helping people who are starving, or trying to save our planet.'

Emma: 'Yes, you are right. It's easy to forget some of those issues when we are going about our day-to-day lives. It's important to remind people why they should support charities. We all need to do more.'

> Emma adapts her comments to suit the situation. This time, she does not use humour or a light-hearted tone because the subject matter is very serious. Instead, she uses a serious tone and draws a message from Amelia's points – 'We all need to do more'.

CHECK YOUR UNDERSTANDING

1. What kind of language and tone would be best to use in a discussion about an upsetting event currently in the news?
   - **a** Serious
   - **b** Funny
   - **c** Angry
   - **d** Bored

2. Someone asks you to explain a complicated subject in more detail. What are two ways you could adapt your way of speaking to help them understand?

3. Look at the transcript of a presentation on page 27. How does Kelly use words and expressions to suit the situation?

1.8 Respect the turn-taking rights of others during discussions, using appropriate language for interjection

REVISED

You **must** always be **respectful** of other group members during discussions. You should:

- **Listen** when others are speaking. Use body language to show that you are paying attention, such as looking at the speaker, not slumping in your seat, and nodding when you agree with something they say.
- Make eye contact with someone you are speaking to.
- **Never** speak over someone.
- Wait for a pause in conversation before you say something (interject).
- Ask questions politely.
- Respond to or acknowledge other people's points. For example: 'Emma's point about endangered animals makes me wonder if …'
- Talk directly to a person when you are replying to them. For example: 'That's such a good point, Tarone. I agree with you. I think that …'
- Give others a chance to speak. If you keep speaking for too long, or if you keep jumping into the conversation every time there is a pause, you will not give others their turn at speaking. Remember, you need to show your **listening skills** too.

> **Interject**: add your own contribution to a discussion. Always do this respectfully.

EXAM TIP

If there are no pauses and you are not getting a chance to speak, try using body language to show that you want to speak. For example, you could lean forwards and look directly at the person who is speaking. If this does not work, put your hand up to indicate that you want to say something.

Caution! Do not do this during someone else's presentation. Instead, you should wait until the question-and-answer session to speak.

COMMON MISTAKE

It is easy to stop listening to someone when you are thinking about what you will say next. Try not to do this. If you are not paying attention, you might miss important points, and you risk your own comment not fitting into the conversation. It will also be obvious to your marker if you are not really listening to others.

1 Speaking, listening and communicating

WORKED EXAMPLE

Group discussion

The discussion topic is: **how can we save the planet?** The group is currently discussing endangered animals.

The following conversation takes place:

> Amelia: 'Apparently there are fewer than 52,000 Asian elephants left in the wild. That's fewer elephants in the whole of Asia than there are people in Scarborough. We have to stop the illegal wildlife trade.'
>
> Emma: 'That's awful. I can't believe that's all that are left. You're right to blame the wildlife trade. People hunt the elephants for their ivory, meat and skin. Maybe better regulations would help?'
>
> Tarone: 'You both made great points, but I actually think the main problem is de-forestation. Large amounts of the elephants' habitat are being destroyed to make room for farms and cities. It's the elephants' homes that we need to focus on protecting.'

Feedback

✓ Emma acknowledges and responds to Amelia's point before adding her own information. *'That's awful. I can't believe that's all that are left.'*

✓ She makes a short but effective comment, then asks a question to encourage more discussion. She then stops to give others a chance to speak.

✓ Tarone wants to give a different view from Amelia and Emma. First, he interjects politely: *'You both made great points, but ...'*

✓ He then introduces his own point of view, explains his point, and stops to give others a chance to give their opinions.

CHECK YOUR UNDERSTANDING

1. Which one of the following is a polite way to interject?
   a 'Stop! You forgot about this really important thing ...'
   b 'Seriously? No. Here is a better way to think about things ...'
   c 'That's an interesting point, but I think we should at least consider that ...'
   d 'That's wrong. Here's what I think ...'

2. What are two ways to show respect through body language?

3. How can you indicate that you want to speak during someone else's presentation?
   a You shouldn't. You have to wait until the question-and-answer session.
   b Put your hand in the air and wait until you are asked to speak.
   c Lean forward and make direct eye contact with the presenter.
   d Wait until they pause. Then quickly jump in with a question.

1 Speaking, listening and communicating

Source document

Transcript of a presentation given by Kelly about her special interest: Playing guitar

Hello everyone!

Today, I'm going to talk to you about my special interest – playing guitar.

I'm a huge fan of rock music and heavy metal. The first time I heard it, I was struck by the sound of the guitars. I knew I had to learn to play.

The first thing to know about guitars is that there are several different kinds, such as electric, acoustic and classical. Electric guitars are usually smaller, and they need to be plugged into an amplifier, known as an 'amp'. Acoustic guitars are bigger and make a more natural sound, but it is harder to reach the higher frets. Obviously, being into rock and metal, I chose the electric guitar.

Guitars are amazing. You make sound by plucking or strumming the strings, and each string makes a different note. You change the sound by putting your fingers in certain positions on the strings, multiple strings for chords.

I use a pick to pluck the strings. Picks can express your personality, just like your guitar can. My pick looks like this.

(Show the audience a photo of my guitar pick)

I really would recommend the guitar to anyone. It's the best instrument to play because it doesn't take long to get good at it, and guitar solos are the bit everyone remembers in songs. Studies have shown that playing guitar releases dopamine, which is the body's feel-good hormone.

Did you know that the guitar is the second most played instrument in the world after the piano? The problem with pianos, though, is that they are not very portable. And guitars are undeniably cooler. Besides, some of the biggest musical legends are guitar players – Jimi Hendrix, Brian May, Keith Richards, Chuck Berry ... no one ever forgets them!

Kelly's picture of her guitar pick

If you play guitar long enough, I think it becomes part of your identity. In the words of the Queen of Rock 'n' Roll, Joan Jett, 'My guitar is not a thing. It is an extension of myself. It is who I am.'

Thank you for listening to my presentation. Does anyone have any questions for me?

EXAM-STYLE QUESTIONS

If you can, practise the following activities with a friend, colleague or family member.

Activity 1: Presentation

Below are some sample topics for your presentation:

1. Tell your audience something interesting about yourself. Make sure you have enough to talk about to fill a short presentation.
2. Tell your audience about your family or friends. Where do they live? What do they do as a job and in their spare time?
3. Explain how you stay fit and healthy, or talk about your favourite sport.
4. Explain why you made a recent life decision or change, such as moving home, going vegan, giving up smoking, starting a new job, or anything else.
5. Tell the audience all about your pet or favourite animal.
6. Tell the audience where you would most like to travel to and why.
7. Tell the audience about a competition or challenge you took part in, such as hiking up a mountain or a video game tournament.
8. Tell the audience all about your favourite film, book, music or music artist.
9. Tell the audience all about a cultural or religious event or festival that you take part in, such as Hanukkah, Eid al-Adha, Lantern Festival, Christmas, Diwali, New Year, Pride, Bonfire Night, Edinburgh Fringe, any music or literary festival, or anything else.
10. Explain something that interests you. This could be anything, such as how a particular product is made, an event in history you find fascinating, or anything else. Make sure you have enough to talk about to fill a whole presentation. Do not choose an inappropriate, illegal or upsetting subject.

Activity 2: Question-and-answer session / informal discussion

As the presenter: when you have finished your presentation, invite questions and comments about your topic from the audience, responding to each one.

As the audience: after another person's presentation has finished, ask at least one relevant question about their topic.

Activity 3: Group discussion

Below are some sample topics for the group discussion.

Theme: education

1. Should life skills such as finding a job and looking after money be taught at school and college?
2. Should all schools and colleges offer sports and exercise classes?
3. Should vending machines selling sugary treats be banned from schools and colleges?
4. Should schools and colleges stop giving homework?
5. Should councils do more to help students with transport, food and housing costs?

Theme: charity

6. Should the government do more to support charities?
7. Are some charities more worthwhile than others?
8. Should companies give their employees time off specifically to do charity work?
9. What is the best way to raise money for charity?
10. Should every person volunteer to help their own community? For example, litter picking, gardening in public places, helping vulnerable people.

Theme: our world
11 Should all plastic packaging be banned?
12 Should everyone try to eat less meat?
13 Should the government be doing more to help the environment?
14 How can we save endangered animals?
15 How can we save the world's forests?

2 Reading

DIAGNOSTIC QUESTIONS

When you have answered the following questions, turn to pages 103 to 107 for the correct answers and explanations. You will also find advice and support here to help you identify the chapters you will need to focus on.

1. Draw lines to match each language technique with the correct example of that technique. One has been done for you.

Language technique
Rhetorical question
Exaggeration
Rule of three
Direct address
Alliteration

Example
This is the most exciting thing that's ever happened!
What would happen next?
Sale at Tiny Tony's toyshop today!
We offer cycling, horse-riding and lakeside walks.
You will not regret it.

2. Every text has a purpose and uses language to achieve that purpose. Draw lines to match each purpose with the type of language best used to achieve it. One has been done for you.

Purpose
To make people buy a product
To tell people how to make a meal
To help people understand something
To complain about something
To entertain people

Type of language
Instructional language
Critical or negative language
Persuasive language
Exciting or humorous language
Explanatory language

3 Read the following paragraph:

Katie listened to her sisters' advice about job interviews. She wore smart trousers, a buttoned shirt, a black jacket and black shoes. She answered questions confidently and didn't interrupt the interviewer. Tarak, Assistant Manager of Dimble's Great Department Store, gave her the job!

Fill out the table below by writing true or false for each statement.

Statement	True or false?
Katie has more than one sister.	
In the second sentence, commas have been used to separate items in a list.	
The apostrophe in the third sentence indicates belonging.	
The full name of the department store is Dimble's.	
The exclamation mark at the end tells us this is a command.	

4 For each of the following statements, put a **tick** in the correct box to show whether it is a fact or an opinion.

Statement	Fact	Opinion
It is hard to stay indoors when the sun is shining.		
Staying in the shade is a good idea on a hot day.		
Tickets for the festival cost £50 per person.		
Affordable tickets are available from the council.		

5 In which **one** of the following places are you most likely to find the **main points** of a document?

　　a　The image captions

　　b　The subheadings

　　c　The footnotes

　　d　The tabs and links

6 You see the sign on the right outside a clothes shop.

What message is it telling us? Choose **one** of the following options.

　　a　Sold out of drinks

　　b　Shop closed at lunchtime

　　c　This cannot be recycled

　　d　No drinks allowed inside

You will need to use the source documents on pages 58 to 60 to answer the following questions.

7 Look at Document 1. What is the name of the magazine this article appears in? Choose **one** of the following options.

　　a　Document 1: Magazine

　　b　Four holiday ideas you should consider

　　c　Happy Travels Magazine

　　d　Packing essentials

8 Look at Document 2. Which one of the most popular holidays does **not** include breakfasts and dinners? Choose **one** of the following options.

   a   Coastal Cruiser

   b   Cornwall and Cream Teas

   c   Scottish Supertour

   d   Mainline Miracle Tours

9 At the end of Document 3, Nadia says: 'It is vital that we renovate all caravans older than eight years.'

Use a dictionary to look up the meaning of 'renovate'.

Now choose **one** of the following words to best replace the word 'renovate', keeping the meaning of the sentence the same.

   a   sell

   b   modernise

   c   scrap

   d   restoration

10 The table below contains information found in the Railway Tours section of Document 1.

For each piece of information, put a **tick** in the correct box to show whether it is similar to or different from information in Document 2.

Information from Document 1	Similar to Document 2	Different from Document 2
You can visit attractions.		
You will only travel on trains.		
You will not do any physical activity.		
All your meals will be included.		

2.1 Identify and understand the main points, ideas and details in texts

REVISED

For questions about main points, ideas and details, you need to identify (find) information in the **source documents**.

Identify: find information.

The question will usually tell you how many answers to give. If you do not give enough answers, you cannot get full marks. For example:
- Name **two** people who can help with customer queries.
- Identify **three** problems the council has promised to solve.

> **EXAM TIP**
>
> If the question does not tell you exactly how many answers to give, look at the number of marks available. For example:
> - At what time does the shop open and close? [2 marks]
>
> This question is worth 2 marks, so we should give at least two answers. In this case, we should answer with the opening time *and* the closing time.

Main points

Some questions might ask you about the main points of a document. These are what the document is **about**, and they are usually the **most important** things the document's writer wants to get across. There are some clues that will help you find the main points:
- They might be in the **title** (or **subject line** if the document is an email).
- They might be mentioned in the subheadings.
- The writer will usually talk about them a lot throughout the document.
- They might be mentioned in the introduction and conclusion.

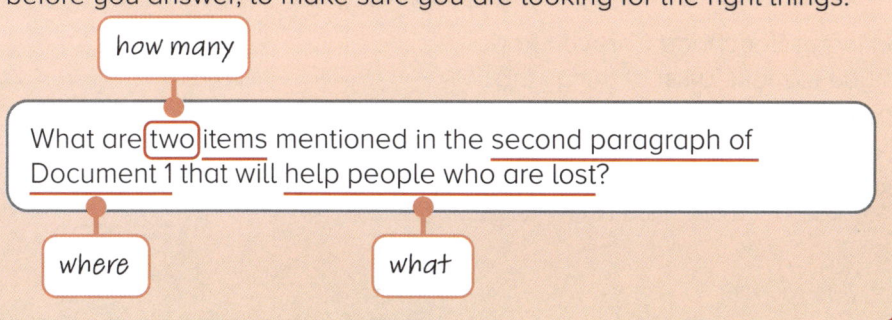

Main points: what the document is about, and its most important ideas and arguments.

Subheadings: below the main title, these are headings that begin new sections of the document. They are normally used to separate different topics and to help the reader quickly see what each section is about.

> **EXAM TIP**
>
> **Question checklist**
>
> Make sure you read the question carefully and check the following things:
> - **How many** answers should you give?
> - **What** information are you supposed to be looking for?
> - **Where** should you look – which document / which part of the document? If the question does not tell you which document to use, look for an earlier instruction, such as 'The following questions are about Document 1.' If the question does not tell you which part of the document to use, you should use the whole document.
>
> It can be helpful to underline or circle important words in the question before you answer, to make sure you are looking for the right things.
>
> [how many]
>
> What are [two] items mentioned in the second paragraph of Document 1 that will help people who are lost?
>
> [where]   [what]

2 Reading 33

COMMON MISTAKE

Do not answer questions using your **own knowledge** about the subject. You must get your answers from the **source documents**. For example:
- Identify one thing that is important to take on holidays abroad.

If the document says that both foreign money and adapter plugs are important to take abroad, you should answer with one of these. You might know that passports are essential when travelling abroad, but you should **not** give this as your answer. You must **only** give answers that come from the document.

WORKED EXAMPLE

Sample exam question

You will need to use the source documents on pages 58 to 60 to answer this question.

What are **two** items Document 2 says you should bring on a Mainline Miracle Tours holiday? [2 marks]

Sample answer with feedback

> One form of ID

Remember the checklist: what, where and how many?

✓ **What?** – an item we should bring on a Mainline Miracle Tours holiday. We have found the correct thing.

✓ **Where?** – Document 2. We have looked in the correct source document.

✗ **How many?** – two items. We have only answered with one item, so we cannot get the full 2 marks available for this question.

To get the second mark, we could say 'camera' or 'charger'.

COMMON MISTAKE

Be careful not to give answers about the wrong thing, from the wrong document or the wrong section of the document. **Always read questions carefully.**

CHECK YOUR UNDERSTANDING

You will need to use the source documents on pages 58 to 60 to answer these questions.

1. Using Document 3, identify one thing that has been added to the caravan park during the year 2022–2023. [1 mark]

2. Document 1 recommends four main holiday ideas. Name two of these. [2 marks]

3. You have just started working at Beachbay Caravan Park. Your manager has asked you to make a list of things that need to be done to improve the park.
From Document 3, make a list of things that need to be done to improve Beachbay Caravan Park. [3 marks]

34 2 Reading

2.2 Compare information, ideas and opinions in different texts

REVISED

Questions that ask you to compare will usually be the last question(s) on the exam paper.

You will need to compare the information you read in different source documents. This means looking for similarities (things that are like each other or the same) and **differences**.

Questions that use one of the following words are probably about **similarities**: *similar, both, alike, agree*. For example:
- What are two pieces of advice that Document 1 and Document 2 (agree) on?

Questions that use one of the following words are probably about **differences**: *differ, disagree, contrast*. For example:
- Document 2 says: 'Dogs make better pets than rabbits'. Give two quotes from Document 3 that show the writer (disagrees) with this view.

Other questions might ask you to tick boxes in a table to show whether information is found in just one of the documents or in more than one of the documents.

> **Compare**: find similarities or differences.
>
> **Similarities**: things that are like each other or that are the same.

Questions that begin with the word 'compare'

Some questions might begin with the word 'compare'. You will usually need to give a longer answer to these. If the question asks you to include examples from the source documents, you will need to give a quote from **each** document to show that the information is similar or different.

Read the question very carefully and make sure you follow this **checklist**:
- **Which?** Which source documents are you supposed to look at?
- **What?** What are you supposed to be comparing – all the information, or just information about one thing?
- **Similarities or differences?** Are you supposed to look for similarities or differences, or can you answer with either?
- **Examples?** Do you need to give examples from the source documents?
- **How many?** How many similarities or differences are you supposed to find?

Look at the sample exam question page 36 for an example of this type of question.

> **COMMON MISTAKE**
>
> Comparisons only make sense when you are comparing two things that are **related** to each other, such as opinions about the same thing, or the main topic of both documents. For example, it would not make sense to compare the main topic of a document with an opinion on one specific point.
>
> ✓ Sensible comparison: 'Both documents are about choosing a pet.'
>
> ✗ **Not** a sensible comparison: 'Document 1 is about choosing a pet but the writer of Document 2 thinks cat food is expensive.'

> **WORKED EXAMPLE**
>
> **Sample exam question**
>
> You will need to use the source documents on pages 58 to 60 to answer this question.
>
> <u>Compare</u> Document 1 and Document 2 to find information about <u>railway tours</u> that is <u>the same</u>. In your answer you should:
> - Give <u>one</u> piece of information about railway tours that is the same in Document 1 and Document 2.
> - Give <u>one quotation from Document 1 and one quotation from Document 2</u> that show this.
>
> [3 marks total]
>
> **Sample answer with feedback**
>
> Let's use our checklist:
> - **Which source documents?** Documents 1 and 2.
> - **What?** Information about railway tours.
> - **Similarities or differences?** It says 'the same', so we are looking for similarities.
> - **Examples?** Yes. We need to give one quotation from Document 1 and one quotation from Document 2.
> - **How many?** One similarity.
>
> First, let's find one similarity about railway tours in Documents 1 and 2. Both of them talk about visiting attractions with a tour guide, so let's write that down:
>
> ✓ Both documents say that you will visit attractions with a tour guide.
>
> Now, let's give one quote from Document 1 that shows this. Remember, when you are asked for a quote or quotation, you need to give the **exact words** used in the document:
>
> ✓ Document 1 says, 'Experienced tour guides take groups of holidayers on visits to all sorts of attractions.'
>
> Great! Now let's give one quote from Document 2 that shows the same thing:
>
> ✓ Document 2 says, 'Visit top attractions, always escorted by our excellent tour guides.'

> **EXAM TIP**
>
> Lots of students find these questions hard, and they usually come at the end of the paper when you might be feeling tired or rushed for time. But you can answer the questions in any order you like. If you find it easier to answer these questions first, start with them and move on to the other questions afterwards.

2 Reading

CHECK YOUR UNDERSTANDING

You will need to use the source documents on pages 58 to 60 to answer these questions.

1. Document 2 says 'a good level of physical fitness is essential' for people who go on a railway tour holiday.
   Give two quotes from Document 1 that show the writer disagrees with this statement. [2 marks]

2. Compare the information in Document 1 and Document 2 about what to pack, giving examples from each text. [3 marks]

3. Document 1 and Document 3 both contain information about caravan parks. Tick one box in each row to show whether the following information is given in Document 1 only, Document 3 only, or both documents. [4 marks]

Information	Document 1 only	Document 3 only	Both documents
There is always an on-site restaurant or café.			
You can bring your dogs with you.			
There are things to do on rainy days.			
You will be near the sea.			

2.3 Identify meanings in texts and distinguish between fact and opinion

REVISED

Meaning

Questions on meaning could ask you:

- What the document or parts of the document are **about**, or what their purpose is.
- To find words or phrases in the document that **mean** a certain thing. These questions will often use words like *mean*, *suggest* or *tell*. For example:
  → Give **two** quotes from Document 3 that (suggest) the shop's items are too expensive.
  → What are **two** words used in Document 3 that (tell) the reader the shop has recently put up its prices?
- What a specific quote or words from the document **mean**. For example:
  → In Document 3, Parvati says branded cereal is 'too dear' to buy. What does she (mean) by this?
  - a Branded cereal is her favourite.
  - b Branded cereal is expensive.
  - c Branded cereal is unhealthy.
  - d Branded cereal is popular.

Understanding meaning from its context

To understand what something means, look at the information that comes before and after it (its **context**). This should give you some clues. For example, to understand what Parvati means by 'too dear', we need to look at what else she says.

Parvati: 'I used to eat branded cereal but now it is too dear to buy. I just don't have the money anymore.'

As Parvati mentions not having enough money, it is clear that 'too dear' means 'expensive'.

Fact and opinion

Questions on **fact** and **opinion** might:

- Give you a list of quotes from the document and ask you to choose which ones are facts, or which ones are opinions. For example:
  → Which two of these statements are (facts)?
  - a Amit is a brilliant actor.
  - b He has acted in TV detective dramas.
  - c Detective dramas are boring.
  - d Acting is harder than people think.
  - e Amit's first film role was in *Blue Skies*.
- Ask you to find facts or opinions in a specific section of the source document. For example:
  → Identify two (opinions) in the first paragraph of Document 2.

> **Context**: the information around something, which you can use to understand its meaning.
>
> **Fact**: something that can be proved true through observation or science/research. For example, if your friend says 'It's raining outside', you can look out of the window to see if this is true.
>
> **Opinion**: a view, belief or judgement. It is not possible to prove that opinions are true or false because they differ from person to person (for example, 'Coffee tastes great').

COMMON MISTAKE

If you are asked to find facts or opinions in one paragraph of the document, **do not** write out the whole paragraph or large chunks of the text. You should **only** write out the fact or opinion you have found. If you quote a few sentences that contain several facts and opinions, the marker will not be able to tell if you have correctly found a fact or opinion. This means you might not get any marks. For example:

✓ Fact: 'Joe is 17 years old'.

✗ Fact: 'Joe is 17 years old and he's already a talented artist. His amazing paintings are guaranteed to impress you. The paintings will be on display from Monday.'

This quote contains facts but also lots of opinions. It is impossible to tell if we have correctly identified a fact. (Facts: Joe is 17 years old. The paintings will be on display from Monday. Opinions: He's already a talented artist. His amazing paintings are guaranteed to impress you.)

COMMON MISTAKE

It is very unlikely that a question will ask for your own opinion on a topic, so do not answer with this. Instead, you need to look for opinions **within** the source document.

WORKED EXAMPLE

Sample exam question

You will need to use the source documents on pages 58 to 60 to answer this question.

Use the information in Document 1 to decide whether each statement is fact or opinion.
Put a tick in the correct box.   [4 marks]

Statement	Fact	Opinion
You will have the chance to use equipment.		
In fact, sightseeing by train is fun for everyone.		
There's not much to do in bad weather.		
You can take part in group projects.		

Sample answer with feedback

Statement	Fact	Opinion
✓ You will have the chance to use equipment.	✓	
✗ In fact, sightseeing by train is fun for everyone.	✓	
✗ There's not much to do in bad weather.	✓	✓
✓ You can take part in group projects.	✓	

You will have the chance to use equipment.

This is a **fact**. It can be proved true or false by going on the holiday and seeing if there is special equipment to use. This is not a personal opinion that differs from person to person.

2 Reading 39

In fact, sightseeing by train is fun for everyone.

This is an **opinion**, even though it contains the word 'fact'. Sometimes, people present opinions as if they are facts, so this is something to watch out for. So, how do we know this is an opinion? We cannot prove it true or false because it will differ from person to person. One person might have fun, but another person might not.

There's not much to do in bad weather.

Both 'fact' and 'opinion' have been ticked in the table, which means this cannot get a mark. We have to choose one or the other. This is another **opinion**. It cannot be proved true or false because it differs from person to person. One person might think there is not much to do in bad weather, whereas another person will find plenty to do. One person's idea of what is 'bad weather' might also differ from another person's.

You can take part in group projects.

This is a **fact**. It can be proved true or false. It does not differ from person to person.

In this example, there are two facts and two opinions. This will not always be the case. Make sure you consider each statement carefully.

CHECK YOUR UNDERSTANDING

You will need to use the source documents on pages 58 to 60 to answer these questions.

1. Document 2 says: 'Fares from £499'. What does this tell us about the cost of a Mainline Tours railway holiday? [1 mark]
   Select one option.
   a. It will cost exactly £499.
   b. It will cost £499 or more.
   c. It will cost less than £499.
   d. Its price will be reduced by £499.

2. Give two quotes from Document 1 that suggest caravan holidays are good for people who enjoy physical activity. [2 marks]

3. Look at Document 3. Identify two opinions in Customer B's complaint. [2 marks]

2.4 Recognise that language and other textual features can be varied to suit different audiences and purposes

REVISED

Questions about language are about the writer's choice of words in the source document.

You could be asked to **find words or phrases** that have been used for a particular purpose or audience, such as making something sound appealing or exciting. Alternatively, you might be asked to **find adjectives** (describing words) used to describe a particular thing. For example:

- Give two words or phrases that persuade the reader to come to the adventure park.
- What are three words used in Document 2 that make the restaurant sound unpleasant?
- Identify two adjectives that the writer of Document 3 uses to describe the shop.

> **Adjective**: a word that describes an object, person, place or thing (for example, beautiful, red, heavy, clever, exciting).
>
> **Language techniques/features**: different ways of using words to create a particular effect.

Language techniques

Some questions will be about language techniques (sometimes called language features). These are different ways that language can be used to make a document more interesting or appealing.

You should be able to recognise specific language techniques being used in the document, such as:

- rhetorical questions
- question and answer
- rule of three
- alliteration
- humour / jokes / puns
- direct address

There are many more possible techniques. See how many you can list, then turn to page 99 to see how many you found on our list.

You might be given a list of language techniques and be asked to tick which ones appear in the document. Alternatively, you could be asked to give an example of a specific technique being used in the document — see the worked example on page 42.

> **EXAM TIP**
>
> Make sure you pay attention to the number of words or phrases you are supposed to find, or the number of options you are supposed to select. Make sure you know which document and which section you are supposed to look at.

2 Reading 41

WORKED EXAMPLE

Sample exam question

You will need to use the source documents on pages 58 to 60 to answer this question.

The writer of Document 1 uses language features to talk about art holidays. Give one quotation for each of the following features:
- a rule of three [1 mark]
- b rhetorical question [1 mark]

Sample answer with feedback

✓ a *group projects, art classes and workshops*
   This is a correct example of rule of three, and it comes from the correct part of the document.

✗ b *What does it involve?*
   This is a rhetorical question, but unfortunately it comes from the wrong section of the source document. We are supposed to be looking at **art holidays**, but this example is from the section about railway tours.

COMMON MISTAKE

If you are asked to give examples of language techniques being used in the text, make sure you give a **quote** that comes from the **source document**.

Do not:
- ✗ make up your own example
- ✗ explain what the document is about
- ✗ explain why the language technique has been used
- ✗ answer with layout techniques such as bold, bullet points or subheadings.

CHECK YOUR UNDERSTANDING

You will need to use the source documents on pages 58 to 60 to answer these questions.

1. Document 2 uses language features to persuade people to book a Mainline Miracle Tours holiday. Which two of these language features are used? [2 marks]
   - a rhetorical questions
   - b repeating words
   - c direct address
   - d quoting experts
   - e alliteration
   - f telling jokes
2. What are two words used in the recommendations section of Document 3 that give a sense of urgency? [2 marks]
3. Identify two adjectives that the writer of Document 1 uses to describe the things you can see on a railway tour holiday. [2 marks]

2 Reading

2.5 Use reference materials and appropriate strategies (e.g. using knowledge of different word types) for a range of purposes, including to find the meaning of words

REVISED

This objective is tested in two different ways. You could be asked to:
- Find the meaning of a word by using a dictionary.
- Find information in different areas of the source document, such as tables, boxes, footnotes, picture captions, subheadings or by following asterisks (these symbols *).

Dictionary questions

These are usually easy to spot because they will advise you to use a dictionary. They may ask you to give the meaning of a word or to choose the correct meaning from a list of different options. For example:

- You are advised to use a dictionary for this question.

    Document 1 says: 'the project would be feasible if properly funded'. What does the word 'feasible' mean in this quotation?

    a   popular
    b   rewarding
    c   expensive
    d   possible

Alternatively, you could be asked to replace a word with a different word that keeps the meaning of the sentence the same. For example:

- In Document 3 the writer says, 'I was in a quandary over what to do'. Give one word to replace 'quandary' as used in this context.

    You may use a dictionary to help you answer this question.

When answering these, read back over the sentence with your new word in place, to make sure the sentence still makes sense.

Non-dictionary questions

The aim of these questions is to get you to use **reference materials** in the source document. This could be finding information in tables, boxes, picture captions, subheadings or other places. Or, you might have to follow a **footnote** or **asterisks** to get more information.

> **Reference materials**: anything that provides extra information, such as a key (which explains the meaning of different symbols), a caption (which gives extra information about an image), or a glossary (which gives meanings of words).
>
> **Footnote**: a small number next to a word, like this[1]. It directs the reader to more information at the bottom of the page. Look at the bottom of this page for an example.
>
> **Asterisk**: a symbol that looks like this*. It is used to point the reader to more information elsewhere, usually at the bottom of the page. Look at the bottom of this page for an example.

> **EXAM TIP**
>
> There may not be a dictionary question on every paper, so don't panic if you don't see one.

> **EXAM TIP**
>
> Even if the question does not advise you to use a dictionary, you can use a dictionary at any time to look up a word you don't know.

* You have correctly followed this asterisk.
[1] You have correctly followed this footnote.

2 Reading

See the worked example below for more guidance on answering non-dictionary questions.

> **WORKED EXAMPLE**
>
> **Sample exam question**
>
> You will need to use the source documents on pages 58 to 60 to answer this question.
>
> Which one of the three most popular holidays in Document 2 includes special rates for families? [1 mark]
>
> **Sample answer with feedback**
>
> ✓ 2, Cornwall and Cream Teas.
>
> To find the answer, first look at the source document for any mention of the three most popular holidays. There it is, under the subheading 'Our most popular holidays'.
>
> But none of those holidays mention special rates for families.
>
> Let's try looking for information about special rates for families. It's in the box at the bottom left, next to a symbol that looks like two adults and two children. Great! Now we know that this symbol means 'special family rates available'.
>
> So, let's go back to the section about the most popular holidays and look for this symbol. There it is, under '2, Cornwall and Cream Teas'. None of the other holidays have this symbol, so '2, Cornwall and Cream Teas' must be the answer.

> **CHECK YOUR UNDERSTANDING**
>
> You will need to use the source documents on pages 58 to 60 to answer these questions.
>
> 1. You are advised to use a dictionary for this question.
>   Document 2 says: 'Be greeted on arrival with a complimentary cocktail.'
>   What does the word 'complimentary' mean in this quotation? [1 mark]
>   - a favourable
>   - b special
>   - c good
>   - d free
>
> 2. You may use a dictionary to answer this question.
>   - a 'Mainline Miracle Tours offers railway tours to a plethora of places across the UK.'
>   Give one word or phrase to replace 'plethora' that keeps the meaning of this quotation the same. [1 mark]
>   - b 'always escorted by our excellent tour guides.'
>   Give one word or phrase to replace 'escorted' that keeps the meaning of this quotation the same. [1 mark]
>
> 3. How much is the single traveller supplement for Mainline Miracle Tours holidays? [1 mark]

2.6 Understand organisational and structural features and use them to locate relevant information (e.g. index, menus, subheadings, paragraphs) in a range of straightforward texts

REVISED

Questions about **organisational and structural features** are about the **layout** of the document. You will need to be able to identify different layout features that are used to **organise information** and to help the reader understand the document. These include:

- title
- subheadings
- paragraphs
- bullet points
- bold text
- text boxes and borders.

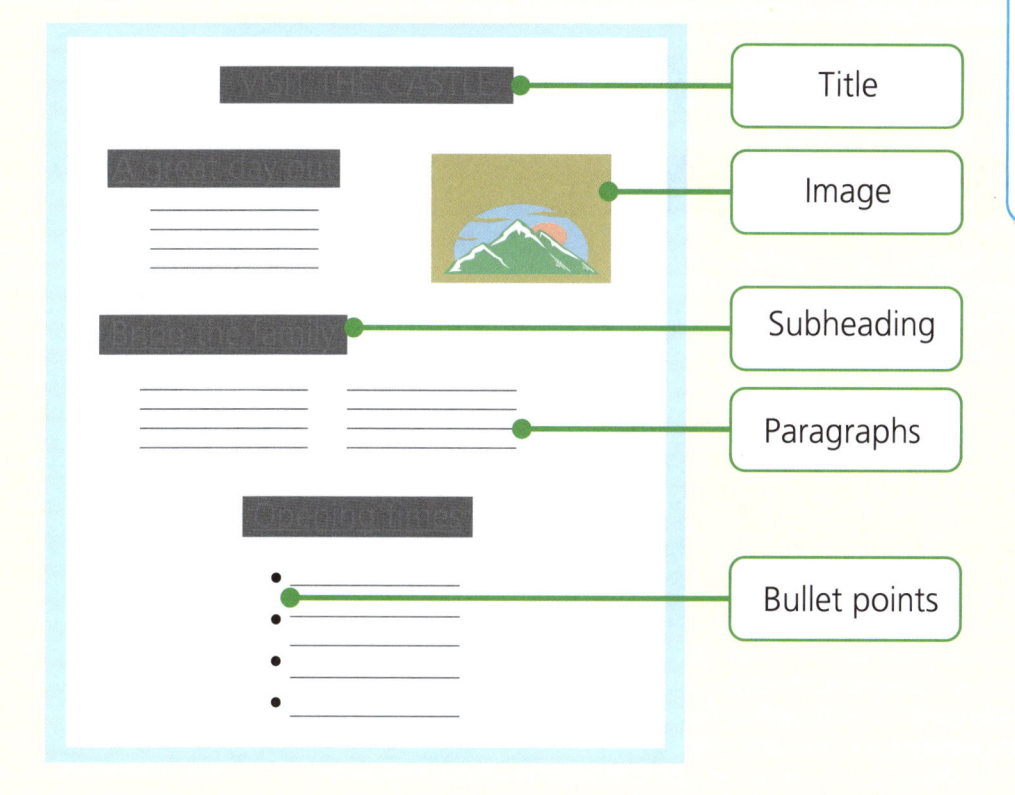

> **Organisational and structural features**: the ways in which the document has been laid out to help the reader find and understand information.
>
> **Paragraph**: a section of writing, at least one sentence long but usually several sentences, which is all on one topic or making one point. A new paragraph starts on a new line.

[Diagram showing a document layout with labels pointing to: Title, Image, Subheading, Paragraphs, Bullet points]

There are many more layout features that might be used. See how many you can list, then turn to page 99 to see how many you found from our list.

Most questions will ask you to name layout or organisational features that help the reader **find specific information**. For example:

- What organisational feature is used to explain the steps of putting the furniture together?
- Give two layout features that help the reader to find the shop's contact number.

2 Reading   45

> **COMMON MISTAKE**
>
> Remember, you need to answer with layout features that help you to locate the **specific information** mentioned in the question. You will not get marks for naming layout features that do not do this, even if they are found in the document. For example:
> - Name one layout feature used in this section that helps the reader find information about a common mistake.
>
> ✓ 'Subheading' or 'box' are good answers you could give.
>
> ✗ 'Bullet points' and 'image' are incorrect answers. Both are found in this section, but they **do not help the reader find information on a common mistake**.

> **COMMON MISTAKE**
>
> Make sure you **do not answer with language features** (for example, metaphors) instead of layout features. Remember, language is about the words and how they are used. Organisational features and layout features are about the way the document **looks** and is **structured**.

> **EXAM TIP**
>
> Watch out for any **extra instructions** in the question, such as the words '**apart from**' or '**other**'. For example:
>
> Apart from paragraphs, name one layout feature that makes it easier to find information on returning items.
>
> ✗ You would get no marks for answering this with 'paragraphs'.
>
> Subheadings have been used to show the different delivery options. Name one other organisational feature used for this purpose.
>
> ✗ You would get no marks for answering with 'subheadings'.

Sections and subheadings

Some questions might ask you to give the subheading of the **section** that tells you about a particular thing. For example:

- Give the subheading of the section that tells you about the history of the shop.
- Which section mentions the history of the shop?

You need to find the correct section of the document (in this case, the section that talks about the history of the shop), then write out the subheading that begins that section.

WORKED EXAMPLE

Sample exam question

You will need to use the source documents on pages 58 to 60 to answer this question.

Use Document 1.
- a What organisational feature is used to show the different items you should take on holiday? [1 mark]
- b Which section mentions holidays on trains? [1 mark]

Sample answer with feedback

✓ a Bullet points

✗ b Packing essentials

The answer to part a is correct. In Document 1, bullet points are used to separate each item the document suggests we should take on holiday.

The answer to part b is incorrect. 'Packing essentials' is the section that tells us about what items we should take on holiday. However, the question asked which section mentions **holidays on trains**. So, the correct answer is 'Railway tours'.

Make sure you read every question **very carefully** before answering.

CHECK YOUR UNDERSTANDING

You will need to use the source documents on pages 58 to 60 to answer these questions.

1. Look at Document 2. Give two layout features that help the reader to find information on what customers thought of Mainline Miracle Tours. [2 marks]

2. Document 3 uses subheadings.
   - a Give the subheading of the section that tells you about things the caravan park did well. [1 mark]
   - b Give the subheading of the section that tells you about actions the caravan park should take in the future. [1 mark]

3. Use Document 2.
   - a What is the name of a famous railway bridge? [1 mark]
   - b Which organisational feature helped you find this information? [1 mark]

2 Reading

2.7 Infer from images meanings not explicit in the accompanying text

REVISED

At least one of the source documents will contain images, which could be photographs, drawings, cartoons, symbols, signs or diagrams. They could be found anywhere in the document. They could be in black-and-white or full colour.

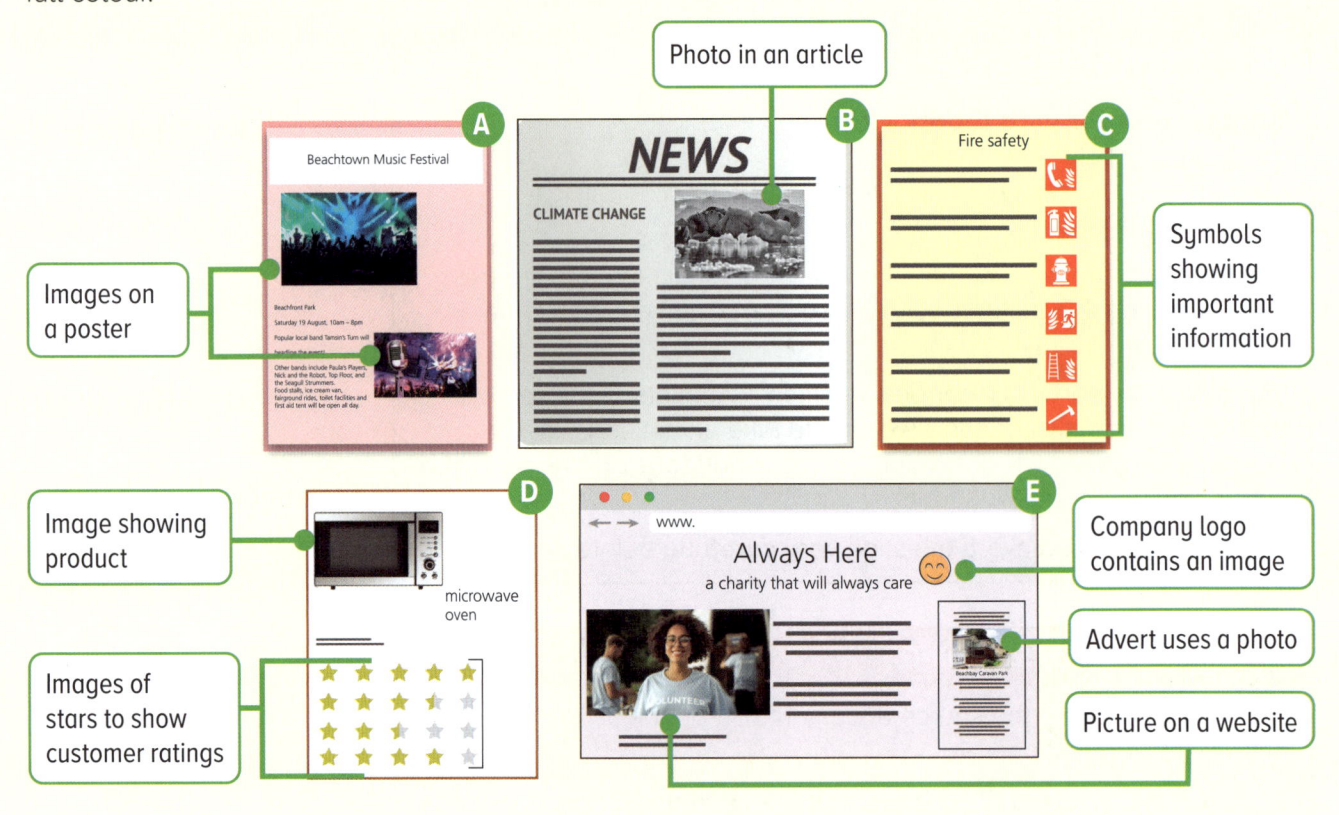

- **A** Images on a poster
- **B** Photo in an article
- **C** Symbols showing important information
- **D** Image showing product / Images of stars to show customer ratings
- **E** Company logo contains an image / Advert uses a photo / Picture on a website

Questions could ask about one image or several images.

Most questions will ask **what** the images show, suggest, mean or tell the reader, or they might ask **why** that image has been used in the document. These questions are usually multiple choice, which means you will need to choose one or more correct answers from a list of different options. For example:

- What does the photograph in Document 1 tell you about the college?
    - a   It teaches students how to drive.
    - b   It has space for students and staff to park their cars.
    - c   It will sell students' and staff members' old cars.
    - d   It is close to good public transport services.

When answering these questions, remember that you are supposed to infer meaning from the image. This means you are looking for what the **image** suggests, **not** what the text (the words in the document) tells you. The image will always show or suggest something that **is not in the text** of the source document.

> **Infer**: work out the meaning of something that is not stated directly.

Questions that ask you to choose an image

Some questions might ask you **which image** in the document tells the reader a particular thing. For example:

- Which image on page 48 shows the reader what a webpage looks like?

   Image E ✓ This is the only image that shows a webpage.

Questions that don't mention images

As we have seen, most questions include the word '**image**', '**picture**' or '**photo**'. However, some questions might **not** tell you they are about the images. They could simply ask you for information from the document. This means that if you are struggling to find the answer to a question, you might need to look at the images for the answer. Here is an example:

Work Site Safety

It is vital all staff follow these safety rules. You MUST:
- Stay out of areas marked with hazard signs.
- Stand at least two metres clear of any machine.
- Walk and NEVER run while on site.
- Follow all instructions given by the security team.

- What should you always wear while on the work site?

The correct answer to this question is 'hard hat' or 'safety hat'. ✓ But if you only look in the text, you will not find the answer. The answer comes from the **image**.

> **COMMON MISTAKE**
>
> It is easy to lose marks on a multiple-choice question by selecting the wrong number of options. You **must** read the question carefully to see how many options you are expected to choose. If you change your mind, clearly cross out your first tick so that the marker does not think you have chosen too many answers.

> **EXAM TIP**
>
> If you are struggling to find the correct answer to a multiple-choice question, first try ruling out any options you know are **not** correct. You may be able to find the right answer by getting rid of the wrong ones.

2 Reading 49

WORKED EXAMPLE

Sample exam question

You will need to use the source documents on pages 58 to 60 to answer this question.

What does the first image in Document 1 tell the reader about stargazing holidays? [1 mark]
- a   It suggests the holidays can be enjoyed alone.
- b   It warns us it is not possible to stargaze in groups.
- c   It tells us that the holidays include using equipment.
- d   It shows us the kind of art that can be created on the holiday.

Sample answer with feedback

✔ a   It suggests that the holidays can be enjoyed alone.

The image shows one person looking up at a night sky full of stars. They appear to be stargazing alone. The image seems beautiful and peaceful, and there is no sign that the person is experiencing anything negative. Therefore, stargazing holidays can be enjoyed alone.

If you struggled with this question, remember that you can also find the correct answer by getting rid of the wrong answers.

Answer b cannot be correct. First, the image does not suggest it is impossible to stargaze in groups. All we see is someone stargazing on their own. This tells us it is possible to stargaze alone, but it does not give us any information about groups. There is another clue that this cannot be the right answer. The text has already told us that it is possible to stargaze in groups. The image is unlikely to tell us the opposite of what the text says.

Answer c is also not correct. The text does tell us that the holidays include using equipment, but the question is asking what the image tells us, not what the text tells us. The image does not show any equipment, so this cannot be the right answer.

Could answer d be correct? No. The image does not show anyone creating art. The image is included in the section about stargazing holidays, and these holidays are not about creating art.

So, if b, c and d are not correct, then the answer must be a.

CHECK YOUR UNDERSTANDING

You will need to use the source documents on pages 58 to 60 to answer these questions.

1   What do the pictures in Document 2 tell us about the popular holidays offered by Mainline Miracle Tours?
    Select **two** answers. [2 marks]
    - a   Holidays will include overnight stays in castles.
    - b   All meals will be included in the price of the holiday.
    - c   Food is sometimes served on the train.
    - d   Customers will sleep on the train instead of in hotels.
    - e   Holidays may include visits to beaches and castles.
    - f   Holidays can last between 3 and 14 days.
2   Look at Document 3. Which image suggests that Customer A's complaint is not true? [1 mark]
3   Look at Document 2. Which customer enjoyed their holiday the most? [1 mark]

2.8 Recognise vocabulary typically associated with specific types and purposes of texts (e.g. formal, informal, instructional, descriptive, explanatory and persuasive)

REVISED

Questions about **purpose** are about what the document's writer is trying to achieve. Questions about **vocabulary** are about the writer's choice of **words**, which are used to achieve the document's purpose.

Vocabulary: the words the writer has used.

Questions that are just about purpose

Questions about purpose are easy to spot because they use the word '**purpose**'. For example:

- What is the main purpose of Document 1?
- What is the purpose of the writing in Document 2?
    - a to persuade the reader to buy a chair
    - b to explain how to put together a flat-pack chair
    - c to complain about a faulty chair bought online
    - d to describe what kinds of chairs are for sale

Texts are written for many different purposes. See how many you can list, and then turn to page 99 to see how many you thought of from our list.

EXAM TIP

Remember that you need to include a '**doing**' word when saying what the purpose of a document is. Ask yourself: What is the document meant to **do**?

What is the purpose of this advert?

✗ *Car*

This only says what the document is about. It does not answer the question 'What is the document meant to **do**?'

✗ *Advert*

This is just saying what type of document it is. It does not answer the question 'What is the document meant to **do**?'

✓ *To sell a car*

This does answer the question. What is the document meant to do? Sell a car. Other acceptable answers are:

✓ *To persuade the reader to buy a car*

✓ *To advertise a car*

2 Reading   51

Questions about vocabulary (words)

You could be asked about the type of **language** or **words** used in the document (e.g. language that is formal, informal, instructional, descriptive, explanatory or persuasive). For example:

- Which one of these quotations from Document 3 is an example of informal language?
  - a Staff members must not enter.
  - b It is not advisable.
  - c She refused to co-operate.
  - d No way am I going in there!

- Read these two statements from Document 2. Identify whether each one is an example of persuasive or explanatory language.

Statement	Explanatory or persuasive?
The brilliant Swivelswish office chair is still the best you can find anywhere!	
The height of the Swivelswish office chair can be adjusted by pulling the lever located under the seat.	

> **COMMON MISTAKE**
>
> When filling out a table, make sure you **read the question carefully** to see whether you are supposed to write words in the table or tick boxes. For example, if you answer the question above by putting ticks in the boxes, you will not get any marks. Instead, you need to write the word 'explanatory' if you think the purpose of the statement is to explain. You need to write the word 'persuasive' if you think the purpose of the statement is to persuade.

> Formal language: words that are meant for a serious, respectful or important situation. It does not include slang or conversational phrases.
>
> Informal language is the opposite of formal language. It is meant for less serious situations, tends to be conversational, and can include slang.
>
> Instructional language: words that tell the reader **how** to do something.
>
> Descriptive language: words that describe something (tell the reader what something looks, sounds, smells, feels or tastes like).
>
> Explanatory language: words that **explain** something to the reader.
>
> Persuasive language: words that try to make the reader **agree** with a view or **do** something, such as buy a product or come to an event.

2 Reading

WORKED EXAMPLE

Sample exam question

You will need to use the source documents on pages 58 to 60 to answer this question.

What is the main purpose of Document 2? [1 mark]

Sample answer with feedback

✓ *To persuade the reader to book a Mainline Miracle Tours holiday.*

We have been asked for the **purpose** of Document 2. That means we need to ask ourselves: What is the document meant to **do**?

Perhaps the purpose is to explain. Parts of the document are explanatory, such as the bullet points. But is this the **main** purpose of the document? What is the **most important** thing the document is trying to do?

If we look at the **whole document**, we can see that all the information and images in the document are trying to **persuade** the reader to book a Mainline Miracle Tours holiday.

How do we know this?
- Look at the huge amount of persuasive language used throughout the document: 'Winner of "Britain's Best Train Tours"', 'a plethora of places', 'top attractions', 'sublime sights', and so on.
- Look at the description of what to expect on a holiday. It uses statements that read like commands, making it clear the writer wants us to go on one of these holidays: 'See the country', 'visit top attractions', 'gaze at the sublime sights', 'be sure to pack your camera'.
- The writer has highlighted details needed for booking a holiday. The price is big and easy to see. The link to book a holiday is also large and includes a command: 'Click here to BOOK NOW!'
- Every image makes the railway holidays look appealing.
- There are favourable customer reviews included.
- And the biggest clue ... Look at the top of the source document. We are told that Document 2 is an advert.

CHECK YOUR UNDERSTANDING

You will need to use the source documents on pages 58 to 60 to answer these questions.

1. What is the main purpose of Document 3? [1 mark]
   a to inform the reader about the caravan park's performance
   b to persuade the reader to book a holiday at the caravan park
   c to explain how to run a caravan park business
   d to complain about a bad experience at the caravan park
2. Why does the writer of Document 1 use phrases like 'If you're looking for ...', 'How about ...', 'Do be aware ...' and 'What does it involve?' [1 mark]
   a to ask for information from the reader
   b to review different holiday companies
   c to answer the reader's questions
   d to explain different holiday options
3. Read these two statements from Document 3. Identify whether each one is an example of formal or informal language. [2 marks]

Statement	Formal or informal?
Most customer feedback was positive.	
You need to do better!	

2 Reading

2.9 Read and understand a range of specialist words in context

REVISED

You can figure out the meaning of **specialist words** by looking at the **context** they are used in. Context is the information surrounding the word — the sentence it is used in, what is said before and after that sentence, and what the document is about.

> **Specialist words**: words that relate to a specific topic.

For example, what does the word 'spring' mean?

This is hard to answer. If you look in the dictionary, this word has a few different meanings — an elastic object in a spiral shape, a place where water comes up from the ground, a season of the year, move or jump quickly up or forwards, etc.

The dictionary on its own will not give us the answer. We need to look at the context to understand which is the correct meaning:

*'The hotel's staff members are ready to **spring** into action the moment you need anything. Just ask and they will get it done quickly!'*

Now it's clear. This 'spring' is something the staff members can do, so it must be an action. The second sentence tells us this is a quick action. So, **in this context**, 'spring' means 'move quickly'.

> **COMMON MISTAKE**
>
> If you are asked to identify **a word**, you must **only** answer with **one word**. If you answer with several words or a whole sentence, the marker will not know if you have found the correct word, so you may not get any marks at all.

In your exam, you could be asked about any word. It might be a word with several meanings. It might be a complicated or unusual word. It might even be a word you have never seen before! But **don't panic** — you can work out the meaning by using the context.

Replacing a word

Some questions will ask you to find a word in the document that can be **replaced** with a new word. For example:

- The following sentence appears in Document 2:

  Every day, crowds of people hurry to catch the tram, one of our city's favoured transport options.

  Which word in this sentence could best be replaced with the word 'popular'?

> **EXAM TIP**
>
> When **replacing** a word, make sure you read the sentence again with your new word in place. This will help you to see if the new word **makes sense in the sentence**.
>
> For example, you might think the answer to the question above is 'crowds', because crowds of people using the tram suggests it is popular. But wait. Remember that our chosen word has to be **replaced** with the word 'popular'. Let's try it:
>
> ✗ *Every day, **popular** of people hurry to catch the tram, one of our city's favoured transport options.*
>
> That doesn't make sense. That means it can't be the right answer. What about replacing 'favoured' instead?
>
> ✓ *Every day, crowds of people hurry to catch the tram, one of our city's **popular** transport options.*
>
> That works. By reading the sentence with the new word in place, we avoided a wrong answer and found the correct answer.

WORKED EXAMPLE

Sample exam question

You will need to use the source documents on pages 58 to 60 to answer this question.

Look at the first paragraph of Document 1. What does the word 'seasoned' mean here? [1 mark]

Sample answer with feedback

✗ It means that you can still have a wonderful time even if you aren't a seasoned stargazer.

This explains the meaning of the sentence the word 'seasoned' is in, but **not** what the word 'seasoned' itself means.

✗ It means that it has added flavour, such as from salt or pepper.

This is one meaning of the word 'seasoned' but it is not correct because this is not what 'seasoned' means **in the first paragraph of Document 1**. Remember that we need to look at the word **in context**.

The sentence in the source document is: 'Whether you are a seasoned stargazer or a beginner, 'you're sure to have a wonderful time!'

Clearly, the writer is not saying that some stargazers are flavoured with salt or pepper – that makes no sense.

✓ Experienced.

You can get this answer even if you do not know what 'seasoned' means. Look at the sentence from the source document again. It says 'seasoned stargazer **or** a beginner'. The word 'or' tells us that a seasoned stargazer is different from a beginner. So 'seasoned' must mean something like 'experienced'.

CHECK YOUR UNDERSTANDING

You will need to use the source documents on pages 58 to 60 to answer these questions.

1. Document 2 says: 'Gaze at the sublime sights'. 'Sublime' means: [1 mark]
   a dull
   b beautiful
   c scary
   d foreign.

2. Look at the recommendations section of Document 3. Which word could best be replaced with the word 'modernise'? [1 mark]

3. Explain what each of these quotations from Document 1 means about packing for a holiday.
   a 'Packing light' [1 mark]
   b 'these necessities' [1 mark]

2 Reading 55

2.10 Use knowledge of punctuation to aid understanding of straightforward texts

REVISED

To be able to answer questions about **punctuation**, you should know the names of different punctuation marks, what they look like, and why they are used. For example:

! Exclamation mark – used to command, to emphasise, to exclaim or to show a strong reaction such as excitement, surprise, humour, anger or joy.

, Comma – used to separate items in a list, or to separate extra information from the main part of a sentence.

( ) Brackets – used to add extra information

' ' or " " Quotation marks / speech marks – used to show where a quote or direct speech (the exact words that were spoken) begins and ends. They always come in pairs – one at the beginning of the quoted word or words, and one at the end.

' Apostrophe – used to show belonging, or that a letter is missing.

There are many more types of punctuation.

> **Punctuation**: the use of symbols and spaces in writing to show meaning and help the reader understand.

Question types

Questions could ask **why** a particular type of punctuation has been used. For example:

- The writer of Document 3 says: 'I just can't wait!' Why has an exclamation mark been used here?
    - a to give an instruction
    - b to show this is important
    - c because she is excited
    - d because she is angry

Alternatively, questions could ask **which type** of punctuation has been used for a particular reason. For example:

- Look at the second paragraph of Document 2. Which punctuation mark has been used to separate items in a list?

EXAM TIP

If you cannot remember the name of a particular punctuation mark in your exam, don't panic. Draw it instead. You may still gain marks for identifying the correct punctuation. For example:

- Which punctuation mark can be used to show that a sentence is a command?

✔ Exclamation mark

This is the best answer to this question.

✔ !

If you cannot remember the name 'exclamation mark', this answer may still get a mark. It is better than giving no answer at all.

COMMON MISTAKE

Do not mix up the names of different punctuation marks that look similar, such as apostrophes and speech marks. Do not refer to apostrophes as 'flying commas' or 'commas in the air'. These answers are incorrect.

COMMON MISTAKE

One punctuation mark can have a lot of different uses. Make sure you are giving the correct use of that punctuation mark **in the source document** you are looking at. For example, showing excitement is one correct use of exclamation marks, but they will not be used for this reason in every document.

WORKED EXAMPLE

Sample exam question

You will need to use the source documents on pages 58 to 60 to answer this question.

Look at Document 3. What punctuation mark tells us where the customers' complaints begin and end? [1 mark]

Sample answer with feedback

✗ Full stop.

Full stops do tell us where sentences end, but the customers' complaints contain several sentences, so the full stops do not tell us where the **complaints** begin and end.

✓ Quotation marks.

To get this answer, find the customer complaints in the source document. You can see that the complaints begin and end with punctuation marks that look like this ' ' — these are quotation marks, and they can be used to show where quoted text or direct speech begins and ends.

Quotation marks can also be called speech marks or inverted commas. They can be used for many reasons, including to show disbelief, sarcasm, that a word is being discussed, or that a word is made up.

CHECK YOUR UNDERSTANDING

You will need to use the source documents on pages 58 to 60 to answer these questions.

1. Document 2 says: Winner of 'Britain's Best Train Tours'.
   Why is 'Britain's Best Train Tours' in inverted commas? [1 mark]
   a Because the writer does not really believe the tours are Britain's best
   b Because the writer wants to highlight these words as important
   c Because these words are meant to be read out loud
   d Because the writer is quoting the full name of the award
2. Which punctuation mark has been used throughout Document 1 to emphasise positive statements about the holidays? [1 mark]
3. Document 2 says: 'a good level of physical fitness is essential for walking tours, climbing steps, hikes and carrying luggage between trains.' What is the purpose of the commas in this sentence? [1 mark]

2 Reading

Source documents

Document 1: Magazine article

Four holiday ideas you should consider!

Stargazing

How can you see spectacular sights without any travelling? Stargazing! Yes, you read that correctly. Whether it's in your own garden or as part of a group led by an expert, you'll be amazed at the beauty of the night sky. Stay overnight at a stargazing retreat and you will have the chance to use equipment such as specialist astronomy telescopes. There are even stargazing workshops. Whether you are a seasoned stargazer or a beginner, you're sure to have a wonderful time!

Railway Tours

There's a common belief that you need to be a railway enthusiast to enjoy a train holiday. Let's dispel that mistaken idea right now. In fact, sightseeing by train is fun for everyone!

What does it involve? Experienced tour guides take groups of holidayers on visits to all sorts of attractions, from fascinating castles to incredible beaches. The holidays can be as short as one day or as long as a week. All travel is by train, meaning you get to relax for every moment of your holiday! Could there be a better way to see our amazing country? No walking, no driving, no physical activity of any kind – just pure relaxation! Even better, all travel is by First Class, meaning you'll enjoy luxurious seats and all meals included.

Caravans

If you're looking for a more active holiday, how about staying on a static caravan site? You can choose from a range of seaside locations around the UK, which means water sports are available. You can even bring pets with you! Countryside walks and sandy beaches make caravanning a great option for dog owners.

However, do be aware that there's not much to do in bad weather, and no specific activities for young children. On the other hand, you won't have to worry about finding somewhere to eat out, as there are always on-site cafés and restaurants available.

Art Holidays

Are you the arty type? If so, there are hundreds of art holidays offered around the UK. At these retreats, you can take part in group projects, art classes and workshops, like watercolour painting or pottery. Create a beautiful artwork to bring home as a memento of your holiday.

Packing Essentials

Packing light is the key to a stress-free holiday, but knowing what to bring and what to leave at home is tricky. Aside from everyday clothes, you must pack these necessities:

- Toothbrush and toothpaste.
- Camera or mobile phone. Make sure you can access this easily.
- Medicines. Don't forget these!
- Charger.

Page 8, Happy Travels Magazine

Document 2: Online advertisement

Mainline Miracle Tours

Winner of 'Britain's Best Train Tours' for the last three consecutive years, our ethos has always been 'people before profit'. Our customers are the most important thing to us, and that's an attitude we will stick by!

Click here to BOOK NOW!

Fares from £499
Single traveller supplement applies*

Glenfinnan Viaduct, Scotland's famous railway bridge

*£80 for all holidays

Mainline Miracle Tours offers incredible railway tours to a plethora of places across the UK, from John O' Groats to Land's End and everything in between. Be greeted on arrival with a complimentary cocktail. See the country and visit top attractions, always escorted by our excellent tour guides. Gaze at the sublime sights from your train carriage as we breeze through Britain's beautiful countryside – be sure to pack your camera and have it at the ready!

- All hotel stays included. You must bring one form of ID with you to confirm booking.
- Train tickets are always First Class. Some meals provided on select holidays.
- Railway tours do not run January–March due to unpredictable weather and snow disruptions.
- WiFi access and charging ports available on every train but customers must bring their own charger.
- Please note: a good level of physical fitness is essential for walking tours, climbing steps, hikes and carrying luggage between trains.

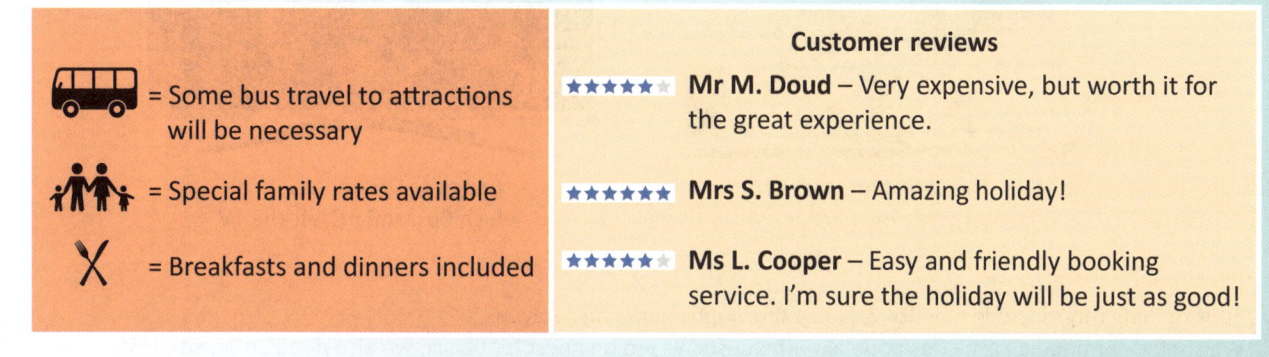

Our most popular holidays:

1. Coastal Cruiser — 6 days 🚌

2. Cornwall and Cream Teas — 3 days 👨‍👩‍👧 🍴

3. Scotland Supertour — 14 days (2 weeks) 🍴

🚌 = Some bus travel to attractions will be necessary
👨‍👩‍👧 = Special family rates available
🍴 = Breakfasts and dinners included

Customer reviews

★★★★☆ **Mr M. Doud** – Very expensive, but worth it for the great experience.

★★★★★ **Mrs S. Brown** – Amazing holiday!

★★★★☆ **Ms L. Cooper** – Easy and friendly booking service. I'm sure the holiday will be just as good!

Document 3: Report

Beachbay Caravan Park – Annual Report, 2022–2023
Report written by Nadia Hart, Assistant Manager of Beachbay Caravan Park, 6 April 2023

Summary of year
There were a total of 1,097 caravan bookings over the year, with summer visitor numbers significantly higher than in previous years.

Park information
Total number of caravans: 20 (all in Model A style, built to the same plan)
All caravans have a sea view and direct access to the beach. Ten caravans also have a woodland view.
Other buildings include the laundry room, swimming pool and entertainment centre (with a space for live music performances).

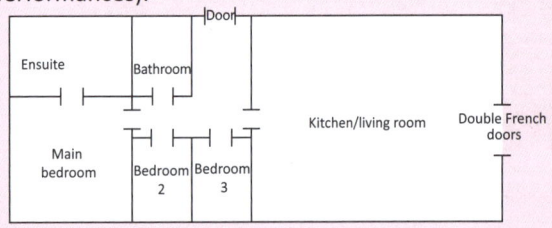

Image 1: Plan of Model A caravan

Image 2: Model A caravan

Changes
A new slide was added to the children's play area, improving the already much-loved facility. Both the laundry room and reception area received a state-of-the-art renovation including fresh paint and brand-new machines.

Successes
The rainy-day activities continued to be valued by guests, especially arts and crafts. In good weather, the well-maintained woodland trails were popular with walkers and cyclists. The water sports classes we offer are second-to-none and were fully booked throughout the year.

Customer feedback
Most customer feedback was positive, although several complained about our 'No Dogs Allowed' policy. Two customers made written complaints:

'The caravans have no outside area to sit with a drink in the fresh air, or to whip up a burger on the BBQ. Terrible! You need to do better!' – Customer A

'It's shocking that you have no restaurants anywhere in the caravan park. Other caravan parks I've stayed at all had at least one café. The nearest eating place was 5 miles away! This is sorely disappointing.' – Customer B

Areas for improvement
One caravan was left in an unacceptable condition by Customer C. Staff did not carry out the proper check before the guest signed out.

Image 3: The condition in which Customer C left the kitchen

Image 4: The condition in which Customer C left the TV

Recommendations
Staff training must include how to carry out thorough checks on caravans.
We should continue all activities popular with guests. Based on guest feedback, we also need an on-site restaurant or café, as there is currently no dining option available. Finally, it is vital that we renovate all caravans older than eight years.

EXAM-STYLE QUESTIONS

You will need to use the source documents on pages 58 to 60 to answer these questions.

The following questions are about Document 1.

1. What is the main subject of Document 1? [1 mark]
   a stargazing
   b packing
   c caravans
   d holidays

2. Look at the first paragraph. Why does the writer say: 'Yes, you read that correctly'? [1 mark]
   a Because they are worried that readers will struggle to understand
   b Because they expect the reader to be surprised by the suggestion of stargazing
   c Because they are interviewing someone who just asked a question
   d Because they want to give positive feedback to the reader

3. The writer of Document 1 uses language features to describe railway tour holidays. Give one quotation for each of the following features:
   a exaggeration [1 mark]
   b rule of three [1 mark]

4. You are advised to use a dictionary for this question.
   Look at the Caravans section. What does the word 'static' mean? [1 mark]

5. From the Caravans section of Document 1, identify one positive thing and one negative thing the writer tells us about caravan holidays. [2 marks]

6. Look at the Railway Tours section. Which word in this section means to get rid of something? [1 mark]

7. In Document 1, the writer tells us that people who go on an art holiday can create an artwork as a memento. What does the word 'memento' mean as used in this context?
   You may use a dictionary to help you answer this question. [1 mark]

8. Look at the Packing Essentials section. Why does the writer use phrases like 'you must', 'make sure' and 'don't forget'? [1 mark]
   a To instruct the reader
   b To criticise the reader
   c To make the reader laugh
   d To sell something to the reader

9. Document 1 says: 'Packing light is the key to a stress-free holiday'. What does the word 'key' mean in this context? [1 mark]

10. Give two layout features that help the reader to find information on stargazing holidays. [2 marks]

11. Using Document 1, identify whether each of the following statements is a fact or an opinion. [2 marks]

Statement	Fact or opinion?
You can choose from a range of seaside locations around the UK.	
Knowing what to bring and what to leave at home is tricky.	

12. Using Document 1, identify two holidays that include workshops. [2 marks]

13 What is the purpose of Document 1? [1 mark]

    a To persuade people to book holidays abroad

    b To advise people how to save money on holidays

    c To inform people about different holidays

    d To discuss whether caravans are better than trains

The following questions are about Document 2.

14 Use the information in Document 2 to decide whether each statement about Mainline Miracle Tours is true or false. Put a tick in the correct box. [2 marks]

Statement	True	False
They claim to put customers before profit.		
Their railway tours run all year.		
All food is included in the price of the holiday.		
Hotel stays are included in the price of the holiday.		

15 Your friend wants to see different places in the UK while on holiday.

Using Document 2, identify two places they could visit on a Mainline Miracle Tours holiday. [2 marks]

16 Document 2 contains both facts and opinions. Which two of these statements are facts? [2 marks]

    a Winner of 'Britain's Best Train Tours' for the last three consecutive years.

    b Mainline Miracle Tours offers incredible railway tours.

    c Gaze at the sublime sights from your train carriage.

    d Always escorted by our excellent tour guides.

    e WiFi access and charging ports available on every train.

    f Very expensive, but worth it for the great experience.

17 Look at the second paragraph. Which one word in this paragraph suggests that the train journeys are smooth and easy? [1 mark]

18 You are advised to use a dictionary for this question.

Document 2 says: 'our ethos has always been "people before profit".'

What does the word 'ethos' mean in this quotation? [1 mark]

    a big mistake

    b company name

    c religious belief

    d guiding principle

19 Use Document 2.

    a What organisational feature is used to show the scenery that can be seen on a Mainline Miracle Tours holiday? [1 mark]

    b Which section lists three specific holidays offered by Mainline Miracle Tours? [1 mark]

20 What is the name of one of Mainline Miracle Tours' holidays? [1 mark]

21 What extra information about Mainline Miracle Tours' holidays does the first image in Document 2 suggest? [1 mark]

    a All tickets are first class.

    b The trains are dangerous.

    c The trains stop for pictures.

    d They use steam trains.

22 Read these two statements from Document 2. Identify whether each one is an example of explanatory or persuasive language. [2 marks]

Statement	Explanatory or persuasive?
Railway tours do not run January–March due to unpredictable weather and snow disruptions.	
Be sure to pack your camera and have it at the ready!	

23 What is a viaduct? [1 mark]
   a   A type of train
   b   A type of holiday
   c   A type of bridge
   d   A type of hotel

24 Use Document 2. The capital letters in Coastal Cruiser tells us that this: [1 mark]
   a   is a name.
   b   is exciting.
   c   is a question.
   d   begins a sentence.

25 Using the customer reviews, identify two adjectives that previous customers use to describe Mainline Miracle Tours holidays. [2 marks]

26 Look at the customer reviews. Which customer has not actually been on their holiday yet? [1 mark]

27 'That's an attitude we will stick by!' Why has the writer used an apostrophe in the first word of this statement? [1 mark]
   a   It tells us the attitude belongs to them.
   b   It tells us this word is a quotation.
   c   It tells us the writer is being sarcastic.
   d   It tells us there is a missing letter here.

28 How many days does the Scotland Supertour holiday last? [1 mark]

29 Which one of the most popular holidays includes some travel by bus? [1 mark]

The following questions are about Document 3.

30 Using Document 3, identify whether each of the following statements is true or false. [2 marks]

Statement	True or false?
The caravan park does not offer indoor activities.	
Water sports are popular with guests.	

31 Document 3 uses subheadings.
   a   Give the subheading of the section that gives you information about the caravans in the park. [1 mark]
   b   Give the subheading of the section that tells you what customers thought of the park. [1 mark]

32 How many bedrooms does each caravan have? [1 mark]

33 Which one of these quotations from Document 3 is an example of informal language? [1 mark]
   a   built to the same plan
   b   continue to be valued by guests
   c   whip up a burger on the BBQ
   d   an unacceptable condition

63

34 The words 'children's play area' include an apostrophe. Why is this apostrophe needed? [1 mark]

35 How many caravans does Beachbay Caravan Park have? [1 mark]

36 Name one room or building that has recently been redecorated at Beachbay Caravan Park. [1 mark]

37 The writer of Document 3 uses language features to give clear information about the park. Which two of the following features are used? Select two. [2 marks]

    a   rhetorical questions

    b   sarcasm

    c   formal language

    d   quoting guests

    e   rhyming

38 Document 3 contains photographs. What information can you infer from each of the following photographs about the state Customer C left their caravan in?

    a   Image 3: the condition in which the kitchen was left [1 mark]

    b   Image 4: the condition in which the TV was left [1 mark]

39 Look at the Park Information section. Give one reason why brackets have been used in this section. [1 mark]

40 Give two words or phrases in Document 3 that make the caravan park sound like it is doing well. [2 marks]

41 What is the purpose of the Recommendations section of Document 3? [1 mark]

    a   To complain about problems

    b   To suggest improvements

    c   To praise staff members

    d   To point out mistakes

The following questions are about more than one document.

42 Document 1 and Document 2 both contain information about what to pack.

Tick one box in each row to show whether the following advice is given in Document 1 only, Document 2 only, or both documents. [4 marks]

Advice	Document 1 only	Document 2 only	Both documents
You must bring a charger with you.			
Do not forget your medicine.			
Make sure you pack a toothbrush.			
You must bring ID with you.			

43 Compare the information in Document 1 and Document 3 about taking pets on holiday, giving examples from each text. [3 marks]

44 Compare Document 1 and Document 3. Identify two ways in which these sources are similar to each other.

You could write about:

    ➜ what they look like

    ➜ how they are written

    ➜ what they are about. [2 marks]

3 Writing

DIAGNOSTIC QUESTIONS

When you have answered the following questions, turn to pages 107 to 108 for the correct answers and explanations. You will also find advice and support here to help you identify the chapters you will need to focus on.

1. Place the **three** essential missing commas in the correct places in the note below.

   > Because we've run out of a few essentials I need you to pick up some things from the shops. Please buy bread milk and cheese. As a way of saying thank you I will make you a lovely dinner. Thanks!

2. The paragraph below is missing one full stop, one question mark and one apostrophe. Put them in the correct places.

   What is your favourite meal Mine is pizza and my sister Emilys is pasta, but our brothers love curries. I asked them why They explained that they prefer spicy food.

3. Circle the correct word that fits into each gap below.

   Playing board games **(are / is / am)** a great way to spend time with family. You can even use games to teach **(the / a / an)** child to read, count and think ahead. **(They're / Their / There)** a lot of fun!

4. In each example below, rearrange the words to make a correct sentence.
   - arrived The earlier train expected. than
   - time breakfast. didn't eat to have I
   - you like What weekend? the do doing at

5. Select the correct spelling of the four words below.

a	becuase	becuse	because
b	definitely	definately	definatly
c	writting	writing	wrighting
d	sincerely	sinserely	sincerily

3 Writing 65

6   Your task is to write a letter to your college principal to complain about the unclean and untidy state of the lunch area.

   Which **two** of the details below would be **most important** to include in your answer?

   a   The different types of food served at college

   b   The type and amount of litter in the lunch area

   c   The lack of seating in the lunch area

   d   The cost of snacks and drinks in the vending machines

   e   Who you have seen making a mess in the lunch area

   f   What subjects you are studying at college

7   Your task is to write an email to your friend suggesting different holiday ideas.

   Decide whether each of the points below should be discussed in the first, second, third or final paragraph of your answer. There should be **one point in each paragraph**.

Point	First, second, third or final paragraph?
Your first choice would be to go skiing.	
You are going to suggest different holiday ideas.	
You would like your friend to reply to your email.	
A trip to a warm, sandy beach would be lovely.	

8   Fill out the table below. Circle which type of language would be the best to use when answering each of the writing tasks, and then fill out the essential structural elements that should be used.

   One has been done for you.

Writing task	Type of language	Essential structures
Write an email to invite a friend to a party.	Instructional Critical (Informal) Entertaining	Email structure: *Fill out To: and Subject: lines. Opening salutation and a closing line. Name at end.*
Write an exciting story about a day when something amazing happened.	Instructional Critical Informal Entertaining	Story structure:
Write a letter to the council to complain about problems in your area.	Instructional Critical Informal Entertaining	Letter structure:
Write a notice to tell people how to recycle properly.	Instructional Critical Informal Entertaining	Notice structure:

Spelling, punctuation and grammar

3.1 Use a range of punctuation correctly (e.g. full stops, question marks, exclamation marks, commas, possessive apostrophes)

REVISED

Punctuation is the use of symbols and spaces to help the reader understand what your writing means.

You need to know when to use **capital letters** and **full stops** in your writing:

- A capital letter marks the beginning of a sentence, and a full stop marks the end of a sentence. A space should follow a full stop.
- A capital I should be used when referring to yourself in the first person.
- A capital letter is used at the beginning of each word in an address. All letters in a postcode should also be capitals.
- A capital letter is used at the beginning of a proper noun – this shows that something is a name, such as David, Manchester and Tesco.

> **COMMON MISTAKE**
>
> Do not be tempted to write your entire answer in capital letters. You will not be able to get full marks if you do this. The marker needs to see that you understand where capital letters are needed and where they are not.

> **Proper noun**: a name or title. For example, people's names, place names, names of companies and organisations, and the titles of books, films and songs.

You need to be able to use **commas** correctly:

- Commas are used in lists to separate each item. You can choose whether to put a comma before 'and'.
- Commas are used to separate the different parts of an address. For example:
  - ✓ Send all complaints to Liam Barnes, Complaints Department, 12 North Street, London, SE30 9NS.
- Commas are sometimes used to separate extra information from the main part of a sentence.
- Commas are used to separate different parts of sentences known as clauses. (For more about clauses, see pages 89 to 92.)
  - ✓ I hate exercising, but my friend loves going to the gym.
  - ✓ After you've read this section, you should practise writing sentences with commas.

This example is a complex sentence. (For more about complex sentences, see pages 89 to 92.)

- A space should follow a comma.

> **COMMON MISTAKE**
>
> You should not use a comma to separate two **complete** sentences (for more about sentences, see pages 89-92). You should use a full stop instead. If you want to join two sentences together, you need to use a joining word such as 'and', 'so' or 'but'.
>
> ❌ It's raining, bring your umbrella.
>
> ✅ It's raining. Bring your umbrella.
>
> ✅ It's raining, so bring your umbrella.

It is **very important** to use capital letters, full stops and commas in **all** your writing. In addition, you should know how to use:

- **question marks** and **exclamation marks**
- **speech marks**
- **apostrophes** – these are used in contractions and to indicate that something belongs to someone or something else. For example:

    ✅ I borrowed my friend's car.

    If the item belongs to only **one** person, the apostrophe goes **before** the s. This sentence tells us that the car belongs to one friend.

    ✅ I borrowed my friends' car.

    If the item belongs to **more than one** person, the apostrophe goes **after** the s. This sentence tells us that the car belongs to more than one friend.

> **Contraction**: a shortened version of a word or group of words, made by removing one or more letters. For example: don't (short for *do not*), could've (short for *could have*), and I'm (short for *I am*).

> **COMMON MISTAKE**
>
> It is incorrect to use speech marks when summarising or explaining what was said. Speech marks should **only** be used for the **exact words** a person said (direct speech). For example:
>
> ✅ My friend Anna told me all about her day.
>
> This summarises what Anna told me. We know that her words gave me information about her day, but we do not know the **exact** words Anna spoke.
>
> ❌ My friend Anna told me 'all about her day'.
>
> Anna did **not** say the exact words 'all about her day', so this is incorrect.
>
> You can think of the speech marks as a kind of speech balloon. They surround the words a person said. In a comic strip, the incorrect example above would look like this:
>
> [Comic strip: Panel 1 – man says "Hi Anna", woman says "All about her day". Panel 2 – man says "Er ... what?"]

3 Writing

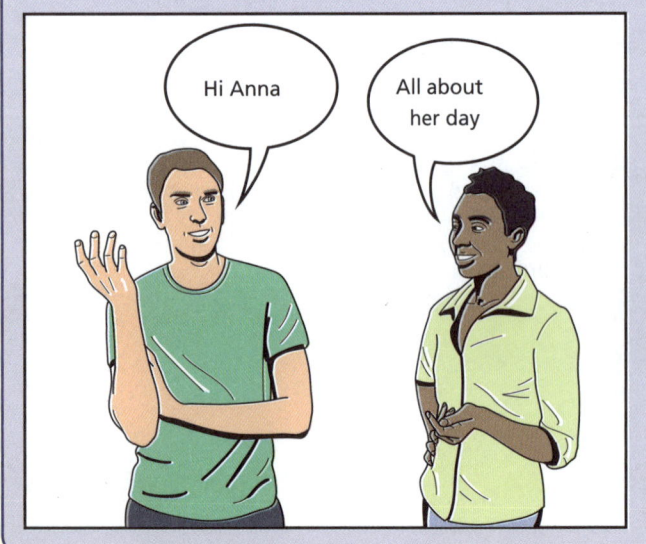

WORKED EXAMPLE

Sample exam question

You bought some items from Jumbles Supermarket. When you got home, you found that the packaging had already been opened. Write a letter to Ms Adams, the supermarket's manager, to complain.

Sample answer

Jessica Smith,
14 Fake Street,
Faketown,
FT14 6JS

6 December 2023

Ms Adams,
Jumbles Supermarket,
2 Jumble Lane,
Faketown,
FT14 9SJ

Dear Ms Adams,

I am writing to complain about the condition of several items I bought from your shop. On Saturday, I bought a bottle of milk, a box of chocolates, some baked beans and a packet of crisps. When I got home, I realised that the milk, the chocolates and the baked beans had already been opened. I don't know how long they were sitting on the shelf, but the milk smelled like it had gone bad, and the beans were mouldy. The chocolates had all been eaten.

This is unacceptable. The box of chocolates was a present for a friend's birthday, but now I have nothing to give her except a packet of crisps. I have no beans for my planned dinner of beans on toast. I can't even enjoy a cup of tea because I have no milk! How would you feel if this happened to you?

I expect an apology and some form of compensation.

Yours sincerely,

Jessica Smith

Feedback

This example shows the correct use of several different kinds of punctuation:

- The **beginnings and ends of sentences** are punctuated correctly with capital letters and full stops.
- Capital letters are used at the beginnings of **names**, at the beginning of each word in **addresses**, and for each letter in **postcodes**.
- A capital **I** is used when Jessica refers to herself in the **first person**.
- Commas are used to separate the different parts of an **address**. There is also a comma after the **opening salutation** (greeting) of 'Dear Ms Adams' and after the **closing line** of 'Yours sincerely'.
- Commas are used to separate items in a **list**.
- Commas are used to separate the main parts of sentences from **additional information** (*On Saturday,*). They are also used to **separate clauses** in sentences (*When I got home, I realised ... I don't know how long they were sitting on the shelf, but the milk smelled like it had gone bad*).
- Apostrophes are used in **contractions** (*don't, can't*) and to show **belonging** (*friend's birthday*).
- An exclamation mark is used to **emphasise** Jessica's frustration with the situation. A question mark is used at the end of a **question**. Both of these correctly replace full stops.

3 Writing

CHECK YOUR UNDERSTANDING

In the exam, you should spend some time at the end checking your answers and correcting any mistakes you find. The following questions will test your ability to find and correct mistakes.

1   There are **four** words in the paragraph below that should begin with a capital letter but do not. What are they? [4 marks]

    Here's how to get to my house. Starting at Sherton Park, drive down Peartree road and turn left at the traffic lights. you should now be on oak Lane. The house on the corner is mine, and i will be waving to you from my front porch.

2   Insert the **three** missing commas in the sentences below. [3 marks]

    There are lots of things to do on a beach holiday. You can sunbathe swim in the ocean, and play water sports. However even beach holidays can be affected by bad weather. If it rains a lot of people choose to go to the indoor pool instead.

3   The paragraph below is missing one question mark, one full stop and one set of speech marks. Add them in the correct places. [3 marks]

    My friend once asked me why I love insects It's a good question. Can you guess what answer I gave him Try looking carefully one day and you'll see how beautiful they are, I said.

3.2 Use correct grammar (e.g. subject–verb agreement, consistent use of different tenses, definite and indefinite articles)

REVISED

You need to use correct grammar in your writing. This includes:

- Using the **definite article** ('the') to refer to specific things. For example:
  - ✓ *Please could you pass me the book on the table next to you?*
- Using the **indefinite article** ('a' or 'an') to refer to general or non-specific things. For example:
  - ✓ *I would like to read a book.*
- Using different **tenses** to describe things that happened in the **past**, things happening now in the **present**, or things that will happen in the **future**.

> **COMMON MISTAKE**
>
> There are many reasons you may **need** to switch tense in an answer, but do not switch at random. This is a particularly common mistake when writing **narratives**. (For more about narratives, see page 84.) For example, the following sentence incorrectly changes tense mid-sentence:
>
> ✗ *I cycled to the park, where I meet my friend for lunch.*
>
> There are occasions when you will need to change tense. For example, after talking about an event in the past tense, you might say something like:
>
> ✓ *We are happy that we raised a lot of money for charity. Next year's fundraiser will be in support of the same charity.*
>
> In this case, changing tense is correct. But you should **only** change your tense in situations where it is needed or appropriate to do so.

- Understanding how verbs should relate to subjects. This is called **subject–verb agreement**.
- Using **plurals** (more than one of something) and knowing how this affects spelling. For example, one car, two car**s**; one sheep, two sheep; one wom**a**n, two wom**e**n; one famil**y**, two famil**ies**.
- Using different **homophones and near homophones** correctly.

There are many more elements to good grammar. You should be able to use your knowledge of grammar to build sentences that work, in which all the words relate to each other correctly.

> **EXAM TIP**
>
> If you are getting stuck on the technical words for the different elements of grammar, **don't worry**. You do not need to remember terms like 'indefinite article' or 'subject–verb agreement'. It is more important to understand **how** to use these elements of grammar in your writing. You will not be tested on what they are called.

Definite article: the word 'the'.

Indefinite article: the word 'a' or 'an'.

Tenses: a way to express time in your writing by changing how the verb (the action word or the 'doing'/'being' word) is written. For example: He ran, he runs, and he will be running.

Subject–verb agreement: the rule that the verb (the action word or 'doing'/'being' word) in a sentence should agree with (match) the subject (what or who is doing the action). In most cases, this is about whether something is plural (more than one) or singular (just one). For example, the verb 'run' needs to change to match the subject, which might be singular (She runs) or plural (They run).

Homophones and near homophones: words that sound the same or similar but that have different meanings, such as: there/their/they're, were/where/we're, to/too/two, are/our

3 Writing 71

> **EXAM TIP**
>
> Check your answers. It is easy to make grammar mistakes when writing your response because you have so many things to think about. This is why it is important to check through your answer after you have finished it and correct any mistakes you find.

WORKED EXAMPLE

Sample exam question
Write an email to your friend to invite them to a party next week.

> **Sample answer**
>
> Dear Mia,
>
> I hope you are well! I am writing to invite you to my birthday party next Saturday at 6pm. I will be turning nineteen and I have planned an amazing night out. First, we will have dinner at the famous restaurant Prestige, and then we will head to the arena.
>
> I buy tickets to see KStar! I knows they is your favourite band at moment, and their also my favourite. I bring are tickets. You needs to bring money for souvenirs, and your KStar shirt of course! The Anna and the Izzy are come to. A concert ends at 11pm.

Feedback

The example above shows good use of grammar in the first paragraph, and some common mistakes in the second paragraph. Let's take a closer look:

✓ **Tenses** – tenses change correctly and appropriately in the first paragraph. The answer starts in the present tense (hope, are, am writing …). It switches to the future tense when talking about things that will happen (will be turning nineteen, will have dinner, will head to the arena) and to the past tense when talking about things that have already happened (have planned).

✗ Tenses in the second paragraph are often incorrect. 'I buy tickets' should be 'I bought tickets' or possibly 'I will buy tickets' depending on whether the tickets have already been bought. 'I bring' should be 'I will bring' because this is going to happen in the future. Similarly, 'are come' should be 'will come' or 'are coming'.

✓ **Using articles** ('the' and 'a'/'an') – 'an' is used correctly for 'amazing night out'. 'The' has been used correctly for the restaurant and the arena.

✗ The word 'moment' needs 'the' before it because this is referring to a specific moment (now). 'The' should not be used with Anna and Izzy as these are names. 'A concert' should be 'The concert' because this is referring to a specific concert.

✓ **Subject–verb agreement** – in the first paragraph, all verbs and subjects match: I hope (**not** 'I hopes'), you are (**not** 'you is' or 'you am'), I am (**not** 'I is' or 'I are'), and so on.

✗ There are some mistakes in the second paragraph. 'I knows' should be 'I know'. 'They is' should be 'they are'. 'You needs' should be 'you need'.

✓ **Homophones** – in the first paragraph, there are no mistakes with homophones.

✗ In the second paragraph, 'their' should be 'they're'. 'Are tickets' should be 'our tickets'. In the sentence 'The Anna and the Izzy are come to', this 'to' should be 'too'.

3 Writing

CHECK YOUR UNDERSTANDING

1. Circle one option in each set of brackets to fill in the missing words in the sentence below. [2 marks]

    I **(am / are / is)** a student at this college. What **(am / are / is)** you studying?

2. Circle one option in each set of brackets to fill in the missing words in the sentence below. [3 marks]

    I have **(a / an / the)** idea. We should arrange **(a / an / the)** party on **(a / an / the)** last day of college.

3. Find **three** places where the wrong tense has been used in the story below. Fix each of these mistakes so that the tense is correct throughout. [3 marks]

    One day, I walked to my favourite café for lunch. I want my usual burger, but they had sold out. I was disappointed, but I decided I am not that hungry. I chose a small pasta meal instead, but when I opened the box, I saw that it was actually a salad. I hate salad! I hope they did a better job next time I go.

3.3 Spell words used most often in work, study and daily life, including specialist words

REVISED

You should use correct spellings in your writing. This includes:
- simple words, such as: a lot, as well, like
- words with more complex spellings, such as: because, definitely, sincerely
- words you use every day, such as: people, know, writing
- specialist words related to the task set, such as: environment, transportation, recycling
- homophones (words that sound the same or similar but that have different meanings), such as: college/collage, whether/weather, aloud/allowed.

> **EXAM TIP**
>
> The writing question itself will contain a lot of words, including some of the specialist words related to the task. Use it to check spellings. You should never make a mistake when spelling one of the words used in the question.

COMMON MISTAKE

Do not use text speak or the kinds of simplified but incorrect spellings you see on social media, such as: ur, 2, coz/cuz, lol, smh, b4, smol. Even if you are set the task of writing to a friend, remember that you are still writing an answer in an exam. You **need** to show that you understand correct spelling to get marks.

COMMON MISTAKE

If you are not sure how to spell a word, do not spell it in lots of different ways in your answer in the hope that one of them will be correct. Choose the spelling you think is most likely to be correct and stick with it.

WORKED EXAMPLE

Sample exam question
Write a letter to the council to request they do something about the litter in your local park.

Sample answer

> Dear Sir/Madamme,
>
> I am writing to make you awear of the amount of litter in Oaktree Park. It is discraceful. There are crisp packets and plastic bottles everywere. It looks messy and it is dangerouse to children, wildlife and people's dogs.
>
> I think you should do something about this ~~imodatly immodeartley~~ as soon as possible. You could put up signs telling people not to through their litter on the ground.
>
> Thankyou for taking the time to read my letter. I look forward to you resolving this disgracefull problem.
>
> Yours faitfully,
>
> S. Patel

74 3 Writing

Feedback

✓ Many words are spelled correctly in the answer above:
- **Resolving, forward** – you may not use words like this much in everyday life, but it is useful to know how to spell them for your exam.
- **Dear, yours** – you will need these words if you write a letter or email.
- **Litter** – this word is included in the question itself. There is no excuse for getting it wrong.
- **Are, this, read**, etc. – these are examples of simple words that you should know how to spell.
- **Amount, packets, plastic, children, people, something, signs, ground, problem**, etc. – these are examples of words used in everyday life that you will be expected to spell correctly.
- **As soon as possible** – here, the writer did not know how to spell 'immediately' properly, so they crossed out their attempts and used different words that they **do** know how to spell. This is a good solution if you don't know a spelling.

✗ However, there are also some common mistakes in this answer:
- **Madamme** – the correct spelling is '**Madam**'. You will need this word if you are asked to write to a person whose name you don't know.
- **Writting** – this should be '**writing**'. This is an everyday word that you must know how to spell.
- **Awear** – the correct spelling is '**aware**'.
- **Everywere** – this should be '**everywhere**'.
- **Dangerouse** – the correct spelling is '**dangerous**'.
- **Through** – it doesn't matter that the word 'through' is spelled correctly here, because the writer actually meant 'throw' – so this will be counted as a spelling mistake.
- **Thankyou** – the correct spelling is '**thank you**' (with a space between the two words).
- **Discraceful, Disgracefull** – when you are not sure how to spell a word, **do not** use lots of different spellings. This could be seen as two separate mistakes, so you could be marked down twice. The correct spelling of this word is '**Disgraceful**'.
- **Faitfully** – this should be '**faithfully**'. You will need this word for signing off letters written to an unknown person (use it when you use 'Dear Sir/Madam'). To help you remember, think of this word as being full of faith – faithfully. For letters written to a specific person (for example, 'Dear Mrs White'), you need to know how to spell '**sincerely**'.

CHECK YOUR UNDERSTANDING

1. Which **three** words below are **not** spelled correctly? Write out the correct spelling. [3 marks]

    Becuase   Sincerely
    Therefore   Choosing
    Buisness   Definately
    Depending   Eventually

2. Circle one option in each set of brackets to fill in the missing words in the sentence below. [3 marks]

    I don't **(no / know)** why we are not **(aloud / allowed)** to use our phones in **(college / collage)**.

3. Find **five** incorrect spellings in the paragraph below. Correct each spelling mistake. [5 marks]

    It's my little sister's birthday on 1st Febuary, so I have one mounth to think about her present. Our parents said that we can all get her one big gift, but I want to get her a seperate present just from me aswell. I think I will suprise her with tickets to her favourite theme park.

3 Writing   75

Composition

3.4 Communicate information, ideas and opinions clearly, coherently and accurately

REVISED

You need to be able to write answers that are accurate, clear and coherent.

> **Coherent**: organised, logical and consistent. All the different points in your answer should follow on from each other in a way that makes sense.

Accurate

Your answer should do what the task tells you to do. For example, if your task is to write a complaint letter, it will not be an accurate answer if you do not explain the problem. It will not be an accurate answer if you write an email instead of a letter. Always pay attention to the task.

Clear and easy to understand

A lot of things can make your writing clearer:

- Giving enough detail.
- Explaining things properly, such as your reasons for thinking something.
- Writing in a logical order – for example, tell the reader why you are writing **before** going into detail.
- Writing in full sentences.
- Writing concisely – this means your writing should be to the point. It should not include a lot of extra words or information that is not needed. You should not keep repeating yourself without a good reason.
- Using correct spelling, punctuation and grammar.
- Using words you know the meaning of; otherwise, you risk writing nonsense.

Coherent

Each thing you talk about should follow on clearly and logically from the points that came before it. Here are some things you can do to improve your writing's coherence:

- Plan first so you know what order you want to write things in.
- Use an introduction to tell the reader what you are writing about and why.
- Make sure you have covered all of one point before moving on to the next point.
- When you change subject, try to make this change smoother by linking your point to a previous point. For example:
    - ✓ *The litter in the park is not the only issue our council is failing to solve. There is also the problem of the lack of car parking in town.*
- Explain your arguments properly. A coherent argument is one that has been thought out and fits together well.

3 Writing

WORKED EXAMPLE

Sample exam question

Write an email to the principal of your college, Mrs Smith, to suggest holding a fundraising event for charity. You should talk about:
- the event you would like to hold
- which charity you want to raise money for
- why the charity is important to you.

The email address to write to is: principal.smith@newstartcollege.ac.uk.

Sample answer A

To: principal.smith@newstartcollege.ac.uk

Subject: Charity fundraising event

Dear Mrs Smith,

I am writing to you to suggest holding a fundraising event at college.

I would like to hold a bake sale. Why? Firstly, bake sales are great fun. Secondly, all the students love cake! It's bound to be successful. Students would make treats at home and bring them into college to sell. We could set up tables in the sports hall for displaying and selling the cakes. All money would go to the Always Here charity.

Always Here supported my brother when he was going through a difficult operation. They provide similar help to so many other people. It really is a worthwhile cause.

I hope you consider my idea and get back to me soon.

Best wishes,

Luke Mosley

Sample answer B

To: Ava500@allmail.co.uk

Subject: email

A bake sale where we make treats at home and bring them in to college.

Always Here is an amazing charity. They really help a lot of people and we are good with their cakes and knowing how to hold events.

If you do this event at college it will be important.

Always Here helped my brother when he was really struggling.

Thanks,

George

Feedback

✓ **Answer A** is a good response to the task. It is **accurate** – it uses the correct email address, the subject line sums up the point of the email, and Luke suggests holding a fundraising event.

Luke's email is **clear and easy to understand**. It begins with an introductory sentence that tells us why Luke is writing. Luke **explains** his reasons for choosing the event and how the event would work. He explains why the charity is worth supporting.

All parts of the answer follow on from each other in a **logical** and **coherent** way.

✗ **Answer B** is **not** a good response to the task. It is **not accurate** – it uses the wrong email address, and the subject line does not tell us anything about the subject of the email. George says the words 'a bake sale' but fails to communicate that he wants to hold a charity event at college.

George simply answers the bullet points in the question without any kind of introduction or explanation: *'A bake sale ...'* What about a bake sale? This is very confusing.

Some of George's sentences are **hard to understand**:

'They really help a lot of people and we are good with their cakes and knowing how to hold events.'

'If you do this event at college it will be important.'

George also mentions things in an **illogical** and confusing order.

3 Writing 77

COMMON MISTAKE

Remember that the person or audience you are writing for **has not read** the question or seen what the bullet points say.

This means you need to **clearly explain** the situation – why you are writing and what you are writing about. Your answer needs to make sense on its own – without the question.

CHECK YOUR UNDERSTANDING

1 You are writing an application letter for a job as a sales representative. Which one of the following options would be the **best** first sentence in your letter? [1 mark]
   a In my last job I worked as a shop assistant selling clothes.
   b I am hard-working, responsible and polite.
   c I am writing to apply for the sales representative position.
   d I look forward to hearing back from you soon.

2 I was going to buy a slice of cake to celebrate my first day in a new job. I forgot to bring my purse.
   Which one of the following words could be placed at the beginning of the second sentence to help link these two sentences better? [1 mark]
   a Furthermore
   b Whenever
   c Therefore
   d Unfortunately

3 Put the five sentences below in the correct order to create a story that makes sense. [5 marks]
   ☐ That was when I spotted the mermaid!
   ☐ After an uneventful journey, I arrived at the beach.
   ☐ My day began bright and early as I started my journey to the seaside.
   ☐ The water looked so lovely, I just had to jump in for a swim.
   ☐ The first thing I saw was the incredible blue sea.

3.5 Write text of an appropriate level of detail and of appropriate length (including where this is specified) to meet the needs of purpose and audience

REVISED

Your writing needs to contain enough information (an appropriate level of detail) to properly complete the task.

In your writing tasks, you will be given **specific details** to include in your answer. You **must** include these. You should also try to expand on these points as much as possible, which means you should write more than just one small piece of information for each.

> **EXAM TIP**
>
> Most writing tasks will give you a number of words that you should aim to write, or an indication of the length required. Pay attention to this.

> **COMMON MISTAKE**
>
> If you ask the person you are writing to for a reply, you **must** include an address to send the reply to. If you do not, this will be seen by the marker as a missing detail. How could someone write back to you if they don't know your address?
>
> Don't worry, you don't need to include your real address – you can make up a fake one.

> **COMMON MISTAKE**
>
> **Do not** ignore the task and write what you feel like writing. The marker needs to see that you can write a response with enough detail to meet the specific task set. You risk losing **a lot** of marks if you write an off-topic answer.

> **WORKED EXAMPLE**
>
> **Sample exam question**
>
> You recently bought some clothes online, but when they arrived you were disappointed with them. The colours did not match the pictures on the website, the material was rough and scratchy, and the clothes did not fit. Some of the buttons and zips were broken.
>
> Fill out the online feedback form below to complain about the clothes. You should include:
> - details about what you bought
> - why the condition of the clothes is unacceptable
> - what you would like the company to do in response.
>
> **Sample answer**
>
> **Name**: Dylan Hughes
>
> **Email address**: d.r.hughes@fakemail.co.uk
>
> **Comment**: I am furious about the clothes I received from you recently. On 9 March, I purchased a black zipped jacket, a blue jumper, two pairs of jeans and a buttoned white shirt.
>
> I hate all of them! However, when I rang up, your customer service representative rudely told me you won't accept returns. It has been less than 28 days since I bought them. I have not worn them, so there is no reason for you to refuse a refund.
>
> I expect you to provide me with details of how to return the clothes, and to refund me the full amount I paid. I would also like you to give your customer service representatives better training.
>
> I am looking forward to your swift response.

3 Writing   79

Feedback

This covers a lot of the details needed to successfully complete the task:

- ✓ The writer has included his name and email address in the spaces provided.
- ✓ He has included details about the items he bought, including the extra information of the date he purchased them.
- ✓ He has included his own extra detail about why he found the shop's service unacceptable, including reasons why he should be allowed a refund. It is fine to do this, as long as it does not take your answer off-topic.
- ✓ He covers the detail of what he would like the company to do, expanding on this to talk about better customer service training as well.
- ✗ Unfortunately, Dylan has missed a very important detail — why the condition of the clothes is unacceptable. He simply says '*I hate all of them*' and does not give reasons.

Dylan should have paid more attention to the **extra information** provided in the question. It says:

The colours did not match the pictures on the website, the material was rough and scratchy, and the clothes did not fit. Some of the buttons and zips were broken.

Dylan should have used this information by putting it into his own words and expanding on it. For example:

✓ *The black zipped jacket turned out to be a light grey, which is very different from how it looked online. To make matters worse, the zip is broken! The jumper is made of a rough material that is uncomfortable to wear. The jeans are the wrong size! This is all extremely disappointing.*

CHECK YOUR UNDERSTANDING

1. Your manager has asked you to write an email informing your colleagues about a work night out to a restaurant. Which **two** of the following are **essential** details to include? [2 marks]
   a. what the weather forecast is
   b. which restaurant you are going to
   c. what you are planning to have for dessert
   d. what you will be wearing
   e. what time they should meet you at the restaurant
   f. your manager's favourite choice of drink

2. Your friend has asked you to write a set of instructions for getting to your house on public transport. Which **two** of the following would be **most** useful to include? [2 marks]
   a. the numbers of the buses that go past your street
   b. the times when traffic on your road is busiest
   c. where the closest place to park is
   d. the condition of the roads near where you live
   e. how to find your house from the bus stop

3. You find the following product review online:

   > *I bought the Bigbrand printer from NothingButPrinters.com and it's so disappointing. It makes too much noise and prints pages so slowly. I returned it and bought a Shinyprint printer instead. It's amazing! It prints at a rate of 30 pages per minute, and it's almost silent. In addition, I can recommend NothingButPrinters.com as a good shop to buy from. They gave me a refund without question, and their delivery times are superb.*

   Your friend would like to know a good printer to buy and where to buy it. Write a one paragraph message to them using information from the review above. [4 marks]

3.6 Use format, structure and language appropriate for audience and purpose

REVISED

Audience and purpose

The audience is **who** you are writing to or for. The purpose includes **why** you are writing (what you want to achieve), and **what** kind of text you are writing (for example, letter, narrative). These things will affect the language you use and the format and structure of your answer.

> **EXAM TIP**
>
> To help you remember these three important things, remember to **TAP**. Ask these questions:
> - **T**ext – what is the **text** type I need to write?
> - **A**udience – who is the **audience**?
> - **P**urpose – what is the **purpose**?

Language

Language is the words and phrases you use in your writing. You need to make sure:

1. The words you are using are **correct** in the sentence you are writing. For example:
   - *I will be driving my bicycle to work.* The word 'driving' is not correct here. It should say 'riding'.
   - *These instructions are sending me mad.* The word 'sending' is not correct here. This time, 'driving' would be the correct word choice.

2. The language you are using is suited to the person or people you are writing for. For example:
   - Writing to a friend: *Hi Steph* (informal)
   - Writing to your college principal: *Dear Ms Heath* (formal)

3. The language you are using is **suited to its purpose** (**what** you are writing and **why**). For example:
   - A persuasive advert for a sandwich might say: *Our sandwich features the finest English Cheddar cheese, juicy plum tomatoes and fresh, crisp lettuce. Why not try it for yourself?*
   - The information on the sandwich's packet might say: *Ingredients: white bread, cheese, tomato, and lettuce. Allergens include gluten (bread) and dairy (cheese).*
   - A critical review of the same sandwich might say: *The cheese was tasty, but that's about it. Limp lettuce and wet tomato made the bread soggy and spoiled the experience. I wasn't impressed.*

> **Language**: the words you use and how you use them, including to create certain effects.

> **COMMON MISTAKE**
>
> Do not use a word or phrase if you are not sure what it means. This is too risky, as you are likely to use it incorrectly and cause confusion. You do not need to use a lot of complicated words to make your writing effective. It is better to use the right word for the situation.

3 Writing 81

Format and structure

Format and structure are the ways you organise your writing and how it looks on the page. For example, titles, subheadings, addresses and paragraphs are all elements of format and structure. Which ones you need to use depends on the text type you are writing. For more about using paragraphs in your writing, see page 89.

You could be asked to write any of the following text types:

Letter

Letters **must** include:

- the sender's address
- the recipient's address
- the date
- an opening that says 'Dear Name' (if you know who you are writing to) or 'Dear Sir/Madam' (if you do not know who you are writing to)
- a closing line that says 'Yours sincerely' if you opened with Dear Name, or 'Yours faithfully' if you opened with Dear Sir/Madam. Remember that the word 'Yours' begins with a capital letter because it starts on a new line, but the word 'sincerely' or 'faithfully' begins with a lowercase letter. Put your own name on the next line.

Ms Maya Armory
34 Brompton Street
Sometown
PN4 7TE

Sometown Arts Centre
6 Cartwright Road
Sometown
PN4 6JX

15 October 2022

Dear Sir/Madam,
I saw in the local paper that you are starting a new Youth Theatre Group. I am interested in joining the group. Please could you tell me more about it?

What ages is it for? Do I need to have previous experience of acting? How much does it cost to join the group, and when will the sessions be held?

Yours faithfully,
Maya Armory

> **COMMON MISTAKE**
>
> If you are asked to write a letter or an email, you will be given the address or email address to write to. Make sure you include this in your answer, and be sure to use the correct spellings.

Email

Emails **must** include:

- the email address you are writing to
- a subject line
- an opening (for example, 'Dear Name')
- a closing line (for example, 'Best wishes', 'Many thanks', 'Yours sincerely'). Emails have less strict rules than letters, so the closing line you choose should be based on the person you are writing to and the level of formality. Put your own name on the next line.

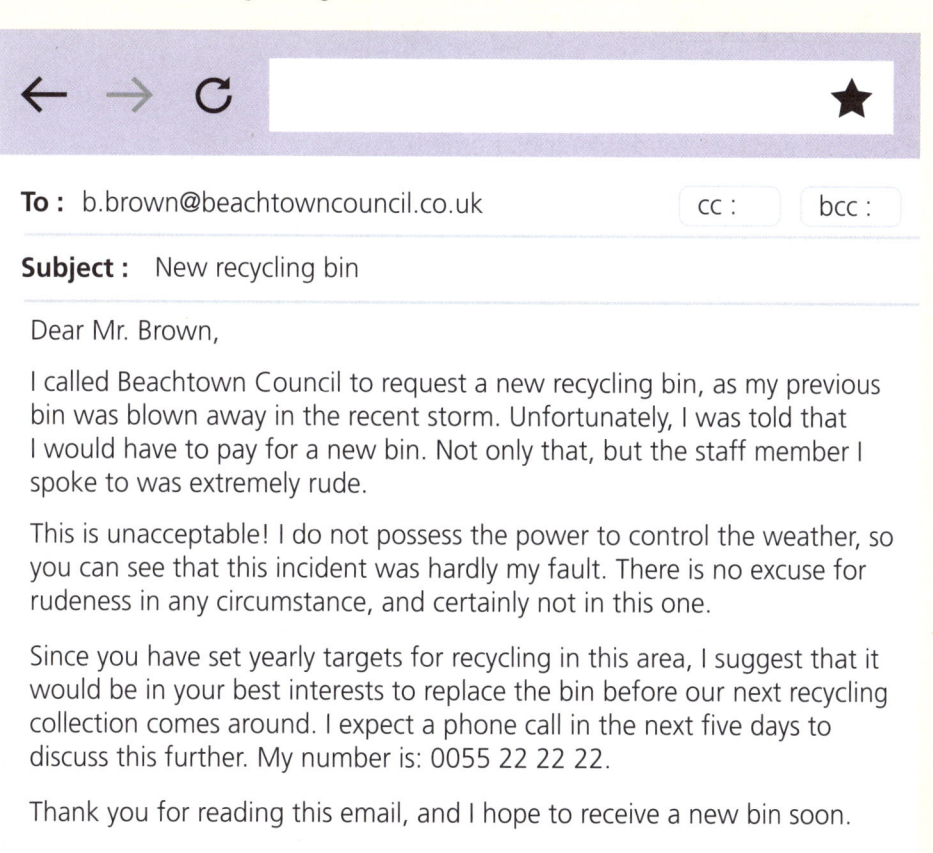

To: b.brown@beachtowncouncil.co.uk   cc :   bcc :

Subject : New recycling bin

Dear Mr. Brown,

I called Beachtown Council to request a new recycling bin, as my previous bin was blown away in the recent storm. Unfortunately, I was told that I would have to pay for a new bin. Not only that, but the staff member I spoke to was extremely rude.

This is unacceptable! I do not possess the power to control the weather, so you can see that this incident was hardly my fault. There is no excuse for rudeness in any circumstance, and certainly not in this one.

Since you have set yearly targets for recycling in this area, I suggest that it would be in your best interests to replace the bin before our next recycling collection comes around. I expect a phone call in the next five days to discuss this further. My number is: 0055 22 22 22.

Thank you for reading this email, and I hope to receive a new bin soon.

Kind regards,
Joanna Smith

Report

A report **must** include:

- a title
- an introduction that explains what the report is about
- subheadings for each separate section of the report
- a conclusion or recommendations at the end.

Look at Source Document 3 on page 60 for an example of what a good report should look like.

Article / newsletter

An article **must** include:

- a title
- a beginning or introduction that explains what the article is about
- an ending or conclusion. Do not just stop writing abruptly. Even something as simple as 'Thank you for reading.' or 'That was the story of my great adventure' shows that you have thought about how to tie up your article.

> **Local Band Wins Gold!**
>
> Tamsin's Turn, a popular local band that many of you will have heard of, played at Beachtown's Battle of the Bands last night. Stunning the crowd, they left to loud applause and roars of approval, and they took home the gold trophy too!
>
> It was a difficult beginning. The previous band, a heavy metal foursome with attitudes as big as their hair, had already won over the crowd. How would Tamsin's Turn follow such a tough act? With humble nods and smiles for the audience, they stepped onto the stage.
>
> If anyone had any doubts, they fell away after the first notes sounded. Tamsin's Turn simply blew us all away. Their songs struck a perfect chord, with just the right mix of clever lyrics and retro sounds.
>
> By the time the judges announced the winner, we all knew who it would be. Sure enough, Tamsin's Turn stepped back up to the stage to receive their trophy.
>
> Congratulations, Tamsin's Turn! Our small community is honoured to count such talented people among our number!

Narrative / story

A narrative or story **must** include:

- a title
- a beginning that sets the scene or explains what the narrative will be about
- an ending that wraps up the narrative.

Review

A review **must** include:

- a title
- a beginning or introduction that explains what the review is about
- an ending or conclusion that sums up whether you were happy or not.

The essential structure of articles, narratives and reviews is similar.

Diary entry

This is another kind of narrative, focused on things you have done on a particular day. It **must** include the date of the day you are writing about.

Eyewitness account / witness statement

This is a kind of report. It **must** include:

- a title
- subheadings for each section.

Online feedback form

This is likely to be a review or complaint. If you are given boxes to fill out, make sure you include the appropriate information in each one (for example, name, email address, comment).

Online forum entry

This could also be called a **forum contribution**. This is likely to be a comment in reply to another person's question or comment. Again, if you are given boxes to fill out, make sure you include the appropriate information in each one.

> **Name:** Joe Bloggs
>
> **Comment:** I think you both make great points, but I have to agree with Maya. Shopping in an actual store is a much better experience than shopping online. I can see the products, pick them up and inspect them before buying. If I'm shopping for food, I can choose fruit and vegetables that are the right size and aren't bruised. If I'm shopping for clothes or home decorations, I can see the exact colour and feel the material. Online photos can never give you as much information.
>
> Chris, I do agree with you on one point though. The cost of driving to the shop or parking in town has to be considered. It can add a lot to the cost of an item when you could just buy it online and get free delivery instead. If I already know exactly what I want to buy, then online shopping is easier and cheaper. For everything else, nothing beats browsing in a shop!

Information sheet / notice

This is usually a short, factual text with the purpose of informing people about something. It **must** include:

- a title that tells the reader what the information sheet or notice is about.

In addition, it is a good idea to include subheadings for the different sections. You could also use other features to help organise the text, such as bullet points, numbers, lists, FAQs (frequently asked questions) or tables.

Fire safety in the office

Fire prevention

Smoking and open flames inside the building are not allowed. This includes candles on birthday cakes, which are a common cause of fires in offices.

Use of a toaster in the staff kitchen areas is prohibited, as toasters can easily overheat and the contents can catch fire. Burnt toast is also a common cause of false alarms. Please use the toaster provided in the main refectory area if you would like toast in the morning.

Electrical fires are the number 1 cause of office fire incidents. If you suspect an electrical fault with any of the office equipment, call Maintenance immediately: 0111 212 121.

Fire doors must be kept closed at all times and should never be propped open.

If you discover a fire:

- Keep calm.
- Activate the nearest alarm by breaking the glass, or shout 'Fire!'
- Leave the building by the nearest fire exit.
- Do not stop to collect personal belongings.
- Do not use lifts.
- Proceed to the fire assembly point and report to the person in charge.
- Check if emergency services have been called. If not, call 999.

Instructions

This is usually a factual text explaining how to do something. It must **separate the instructions** so they are easy to follow. You could do this with numbers, bullet points, lists, subheadings, paragraphs, or any other organisational feature that works. It is a good idea to include a **title** at the beginning that says what the instructions are for.

Advertisement feature

Think of this as an article that is trying to sell or promote something as its main purpose. It needs a **title**.

> **EXAM TIP**
>
> Have you noticed how often '**title**' comes up as an important element? The only text types that **should not** have titles are letters and emails. All other text types either need a title or would work well with one.

WORKED EXAMPLE

Sample exam question

Square i Entertainment magazine is looking for reviews of popular entertainment to include in the next issue of the magazine. Every published review will earn its writer £100.

Write a review of a film or TV series that you enjoyed.

Sample answer A with feedback

✓ Title

> 'Bees in a Boat' – a Review
>
> By Chantale K.
>
> 'Bees in a Boat' is a film released in 2023. While it was clearly made on a low budget, it is high on thrills!
>
> The film
>
> Casting bees as the bad guys was very effective. It allowed for a slow building up of tension, as bees are not immediately scary. When the characters realise they're trapped on a boat with the swarm, it soon becomes clear that angry bees can be just as scary as snakes!
>
> The actors were mostly brilliant, although one leading man let the film down with an over-the-top performance. I feel sure some of these actors will become the stars of the future!
>
> Overall – 8 out of 10
>
> I enjoyed this film. As long as you don't take it too seriously, it's great fun. It's also surprisingly tense at times. Give it a try!

✓ Byline (the name of the writer)

✓ Introduction gives information about the film and hints at Chantale's positive opinions.

✓ Subheadings for each section.

✓ Answer broken down into paragraphs. A new paragraph for each new point.

✓ Conclusion that sums up Chantale's opinions and gives a personal recommendation.

Sample answer B with feedback

(✗) No title. The most important formatting element is missing.

> 'Bees in a Boat' is a 2023 cinematic product directed by Vicki Cooper. It fixtures the actors May Park and Joel Lowe in the leading honours. It runs into a total of 97 minutes. The plot begins with four friends setting away on their boat for the weekend. Nobody realises that a herd of mutant bees is in the boat. The danger improves as the friends try to get back to shore. Critics agree that May Parks did an excellent acting as Val Lee, the boat's author. It uses many low-money effects.

(✗) First sentence gives information about the film but there is no real introduction to the review.

(✗) No paragraphs. A very important structural element is missing.

(✗) No real conclusion. No summary of the author's opinions. No recommendation.

Feedback

Answer A is more successful than Answer B. Let's take a closer look.

First, we need to **TAP**:
- **Text** – a review
- **Audience** – readers of an entertainment magazine
- **Purpose** – to review (give my opinions and the reasons for them)

(✓) **Answer A** is **formatted and structured correctly** for a review.

(✗) **Answer B** has no title and no paragraphs. There is some structure, as it tells the plot in the order the events took place. However, there is no clear introduction or conclusion.

(✓) **Answer A** uses language **appropriate** for purpose and audience. The review is written in a lively, entertaining way – 'high on thrills', 'bees as the bad guys', 'just as scary as snakes', 'the stars of the future'. The informal style will appeal to the magazine's readers.

(✗) **Answer B** uses a formal, factual style that is less appropriate for a magazine review.

(✓) **Answer A** is a more **useful** review than Answer B. For every part of the film Chantale mentions, she explains why she found it good or bad – 'very effective', 'slow building up of tension', 'over-the-top performance', 'enjoyed', 'fun', 'surprisingly tense', and many more examples. She gives a summary of her opinions and a personal recommendation – 'Give it a try'.

(✗) **Answer B** does not contain the reviewer's opinions.

(✓) **Answer A** has no incorrect language.

(✗) **Answer B** uses some **incorrect** and **confusing** language. Calling the film a 'cinematic product' is an odd expression. Simply saying 'film' would have worked better.

Other language errors include: 'fixtures' (this should be 'features'), 'honours' (should be 'roles'), 'runs into' (should be 'runs for'), 'setting away' (should be 'setting out/off/sail'), 'herd' (should be 'swarm'), 'improves' (should be 'increases'), 'did an excellent acting' (should be 'gave an excellent performance' or 'did an excellent job'), 'author' (should be 'owner') and 'low money' (should be 'low budget').

3 Writing   87

CHECK YOUR UNDERSTANDING

1 Look at the following writing task.
  You witnessed a road accident while walking home one evening. The police have asked all witnesses to write a report of the accident.
  Which one of the following types of language would be best suited to answering this question? [1 mark]
  a formal
  b persuasive
  c technical
  d entertaining

2 When writing an article, narrative or report, what should always come first? [1 mark]
  a introduction
  b title
  c your address
  d your name

3 Look at the letter below. Decide whether each labelled element of format or structure is correct or incorrect. [5 marks]

Application for a job — Title. Correct / Incorrect

Human Resources Department,
Dimbles Department Store,
10 Dimbles Street,
DD1 4DS

— Recipient's address followed by the sender's address. Correct / Incorrect

Katy Sanders,
3 Fake Road,
Faketown,
FT3 3TF

Dear Sir/Madam, — Opening salutation of 'Sir/Madam' to an unknown person. Correct / Incorrect

I am writing to apply for a job in the Human Resources Department.

I have never worked in this role before, but I am hard-working and quick to learn. I have never been late for any appointment, and I take my responsibilities seriously.

I look forward to your reply.

Best wishes, — Closing line of 'Best wishes'. Correct / Incorrect

Katy Sanders — Letter ends with sender's name. Correct / Incorrect

3.7 Write consistently and accurately in complex sentences, using paragraphs where appropriate

REVISED

Paragraphs

You should separate your writing into sections called **paragraphs**. Each paragraph should:

- start on a new line.
- be all on one idea or topic, or making one point. When you want to switch ideas, topics or points, start a new paragraph.
- begin with a sentence that explains what the paragraph will be about or sets the scene. This is sometimes called the 'topic sentence'. For example: 'My adventure began when I arrived at the base of the mountain.' Or 'It is important to eat healthily.' The sentences that follow will then give more information about this.

> **Paragraph**: a section of writing, at least one sentence long but usually several sentences, which is all on one topic or making one point.

EXAM TIP

If you have written your answer without paragraphs and need to add them in later, you can do this by marking where the new paragraph should begin. For example:

> When I got to the hotel, I went straight to bed. The next morning, I woke up bright and early to get to the beach before anyone else.
>
> *New paragraph*

> When I got to the hotel, I went straight to bed. *The next morning, I woke up bright and early to get to the beach before anyone else.
>
> *Should be a new paragraph*

> When I got to the hotel, I went straight to bed. The next morning, I woke up bright and early to get to the beach before anyone else.

Sentences

Sentence structure might seem like a very difficult topic at first because there are so many technical terms. But try not to worry. Writing different kinds of sentences is not as hard as it might look. In fact, you probably already write complex sentences without even trying. For example, do you use sentences like these?

- *I need to get my coat because it's raining outside.*
- *After we've finished work, let's go get dinner.*

These are complex sentences. If you can use sentences like this in your writing, you are already well on your way.

Before we look at complex sentences in more detail, there are some terms that will help you understand more about how sentences are built.

EXAM TIP

Each writing question will give you a list of details that you should include in your answer. It is often a good idea to base your paragraphs on these, using a new paragraph for each point.

3 Writing 89

> **Clause**: a group of words that contains at least one **verb** or action word (sometimes referred to as a 'doing or being' word) and a **subject** (who or what is doing the action). A clause can form part of a sentence or it can be one whole sentence. Below are three clauses with the verbs circled and the subjects underlined.
>
> - The dog played with his ball
> - Freya will walk to college
> - If you want breakfast
>
> **Independent clause**: a clause that can stand on its own as a sentence.
>
> - You should bring your umbrella.
>
> **Dependent clause**: a clause that cannot stand on its own as a sentence. A dependent clause will usually explain an independent clause or add extra information to it. It will contain a linking word such as 'because' – this is used to attach the dependent clause to an independent clause.
>
> - because it's raining
>
> If we attach this dependent clause to the independent clause above, it becomes a full complex sentence:
>
> - You should bring your umbrella because it's raining.

There are three different kinds of sentence that you need to know how to write:

1. **Simple sentences** – made of one **independent clause**. For example:
    → I kicked the football.
    → It hit the window.

2. **Compound sentences** – made of one **independent clause** + a **joining word** + one **independent clause**. Joining words you can use in compound sentences are: for, and, nor, but, or, yet, so. For example:
    → I kicked the football **and** it hit the window.

3. **Complex sentences** – made of one **independent clause** + one **dependent clause** that contains a linking word. There are lots of linking words you can use in a complex sentence, but the most common ones are: because, after, unless, since, although, if. For example:
    → The window broke because the football hit it.

You should use all three types of sentence in your answer to make your writing feel natural and interesting. You **must** include **correct complex sentences** to get marks.

But wait. **Where do I put the commas?**

A general rule is: if the independent clause comes first, you don't need a comma. The **independent clauses** in the sentences below are **shown in green**. Notice that these are the main point of each sentence. When the independent clause comes first, the linking word will be in between the clauses, in the middle of the sentence. (See the examples in the first two bullet points below.)

If the dependent clause comes first, you should put a comma before the independent clause. The **dependent clauses** in the sentences below are **shown in purple**. Notice that these explain or add extra information to the main point of the sentence. When the dependent clause comes first, the linking word is at the beginning of the sentence. (See the examples in the last three bullet points below.)

- The floor is wet because I just mopped it.
- It began to make sense after I had revised enough.
- Since you insist, I'll have another slice of cake.
- Although it's late, you can watch one more episode.
- If you think this is hard, you should try doing the maths paper.

COMMON MISTAKE

You **cannot** join two sentences together with just a comma. Instead, create a compound sentence with a joining word like 'and' or 'but', or create a complex sentence with a linking word like 'because.'

✗ I was too late, I missed the bus.
✓ I was too late, and I missed the bus.
✓ Because I was too late, I missed the bus.

COMMON MISTAKE

Do not write every sentence using the same structure. That will make your writing sound clumsy. You must include complex sentences, but you need to include some simple and some compound sentences as well.

EXAM TIP

You do not need to remember any of these technical terms to be able to write good sentences. As long as you can write sentences that work, and you can include some complex sentences, you will be fine.

WORKED EXAMPLE

Sample exam question
Write a story about a day that started badly but turned into a good day.

Sample answer

The Day I Got Promoted

My day did not begin well. The rain pounded against the window as I jumped out of bed. My alarm had not gone off, and I was already late for work. I had an important meeting in ten minutes. Could this day get any worse?

As it turned out, the day could get a lot worse. I ran to my office building, and I hurried into the lift. As it passed the ninth floor, the lift suddenly stopped. I couldn't believe it. I was missing my meeting, and I was stuck in the lift with a complete stranger.

That stranger now started to panic. I had to calm her down somehow. I told her all my amazing ideas for the company so she would be distracted from the situation. It worked!

Example of a complex sentence where the independent clause comes first.

Example of a complex sentence where the dependent clause comes first.

3 Writing

Half an hour later, my luck changed. The lift began moving again, and we were soon at my floor. Because my manager had been told about the broken lift, she did not blame me for being late.

Can you guess the best part? The woman in the lift was actually the head of the company. She was grateful for my help in the lift, and she was impressed with my ideas. I was promoted on the spot.

Feedback

✓ The paragraphing in this story is excellent. Each paragraph tells a different part of the story, with first sentences that set the scene: *'My day did not begin well.'* The final paragraph tells the ending of the story.

✓ Each paragraph is linked to the previous paragraph so that the story flows together well. *'Could this day get any worse? As it turned out, the day could get a lot worse.' 'That stranger now started to panic.' 'Half an hour later …'*

✓ All three sentence structures appear in this story, which helps the writing sound natural and avoids clumsiness. In fact, the first three sentences use all three sentence types.

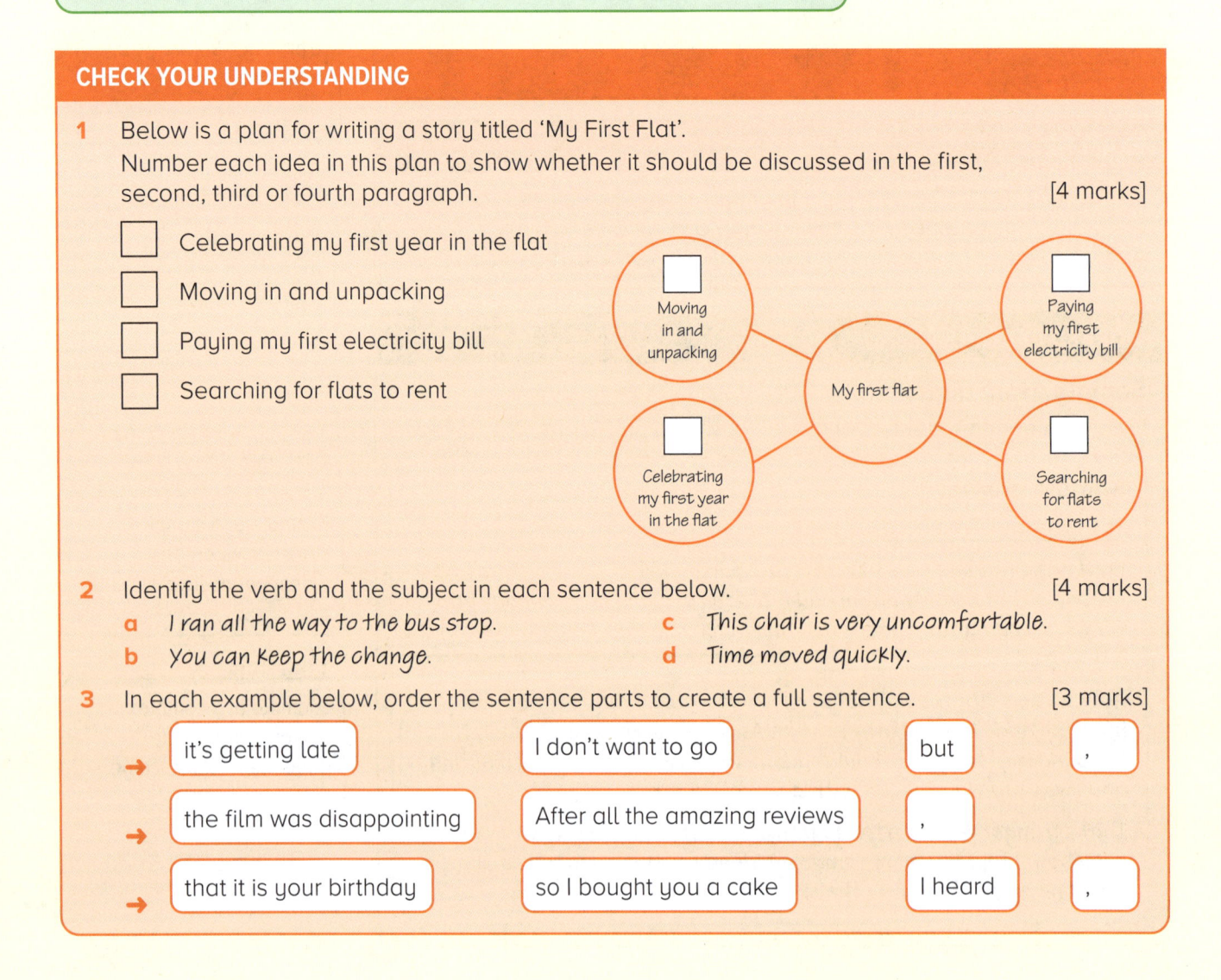

CHECK YOUR UNDERSTANDING

1   Below is a plan for writing a story titled 'My First Flat'.
    Number each idea in this plan to show whether it should be discussed in the first, second, third or fourth paragraph.
    [4 marks]

    ☐ Celebrating my first year in the flat
    ☐ Moving in and unpacking
    ☐ Paying my first electricity bill
    ☐ Searching for flats to rent

    (Diagram: My first flat — Moving in and unpacking, Paying my first electricity bill, Celebrating my first year in the flat, Searching for flats to rent)

2   Identify the verb and the subject in each sentence below. [4 marks]
    a   I ran all the way to the bus stop.
    b   You can keep the change.
    c   This chair is very uncomfortable.
    d   Time moved quickly.

3   In each example below, order the sentence parts to create a full sentence. [3 marks]

    → | it's getting late | I don't want to go | but | , |
    → | the film was disappointing | After all the amazing reviews | , |
    → | that it is your birthday | so I bought you a cake | I heard | , |

EXAM-STYLE QUESTIONS

1. **Activity: Write a letter**

   You see this poster:

   Looking for new Magician's Assistant!

   Local magician looking for a new assistant to help with:
   - magic tricks and illusions
   - setting up the stage
   - preparing equipment
   - transporting equipment.

   No experience or training needed, just a willingness to learn and a desire to bring joy to audiences. Must be able to keep secrets, as they will be taught how all the magic tricks work.

   To apply, send a letter of application to: Miss H. Presto, 13 Sleight Street, Newberry, NB3 9HP.

   Write a letter to apply for the position of Magician's Assistant. In your letter, you should:
   → say why you are interested in the job
   → explain why you think you would be the right person for the job
   → talk about any of your skills or personal qualities that you feel are relevant.

   Your letter should be about 150–250 words long. [20 marks]

2. **Information**

   You recently visited Sherton Leisure Centre, advertised on the flyer below.

   Sherton Leisure Centre

   Run by Sherton Council

   Everyone is welcome!

   Be Active
   We have:
   - Swimming pool
   - Children's pool
   - Squash and netball courts
   - Gym
   - Self-defence classes
   - Dance classes

   Work and Relax
   Discover our:
   - Café
   - Meeting rooms
   - Sauna
   - Children's play area

   Disabled access in all areas. Changing and shower facilities available. Parking only for licence holders.

   Writing task

   Write a review of Sherton Leisure Centre for your community website. In your review, you should:
   → say when you visited and what you did at the centre
   → describe your experience with different rooms, facilities or classes
   → explain why you recommend or do not recommend the centre.

   You should aim to write about 200–250 words. [21 marks]

3 You attend college one day a week. Recently, you have been struggling to hear the tutor during classes because of disruptive students outside. You have heard shouting in the corridors and loud games of football in the yard outside your classroom.

Your task: Write an email to Ms Heath, the principal of your college, to request something is done about the disruptions. Her email address is: principalheath@newstartcollege.ac.uk.

You should include:

- why you are writing and what the problems are
- why this is interfering with your learning
- why your weekly day at college is important to you
- what you think the college should do about the disruptions (for example, put notices in corridors, issue penalties, give students access to a proper sports field during their free periods).

You should write about 250 words. [27 marks]

4 Activity: Write an advertisement feature

The number of shoppers at your town's weekly market is decreasing. Write an advertisement feature encouraging more people to come and shop.

In your advertisement feature, you could:

- describe the market, its stalls and what kinds of things are sold
- persuade people to come and shop
- include information for shoppers (for example, what day it runs, times, location, parking).

Your advertisement feature should be about 150–250 words long. [20 marks]

5 You have started work with a local volunteer group that teaches important life skills to young people. Your first task is to write a set of instructions for one of their leaflets. They need instructions on **one** of the following topics:

- How to find and move into a new home
- How to create a social media profile and keep it updated
- How to look for a job and then apply for one
- How to paint and re-decorate a room
- Any other useful skill for a young person to know

Your task: Write the instructions.

You should include:

- what your instructions are for
- any materials or tools needed to carry out the task
- how to begin
- all the steps that someone needs to follow to complete the task
- where they can look for extra help if needed (for example, online, community classes, in a library).

You should write about 200–250 words. [27 marks]

6 Information

> You attend a party for a birthday or other special celebration. Several things go wrong during the party, including the following:
>
> - Someone falls on top of the cake.
> - The wrong food is served at dinner.
> - The sound system gets stuck playing the same song over and over.
> - An animal breaks loose from a nearby farm and gets into the party area.
>
> This results in a memorable event!

Writing task

Write a diary entry about this party.

In your diary entry, you should:

→ describe what happened at the party

→ say whether the things that went wrong spoiled the party or made it better.

You should aim to write about 150–200 words. [15 marks]

7 You read the following on a community website:

> **Sherton Summer Festival**
>
> The summer festival is back, and this time we need YOUR ideas.
> - What should the theme be? Summer flowers? The beach? Or something else?
> - What food should be served in the food tent?
> - What kind of music artists or bands should play?
> - Which fairground rides should we include?
>
> *Tell us your ideas, and we will pick one winner. Not only will the winner's ideas be included in this year's fair, but they will win a holiday for two to Beachtown.*
>
> Send your ideas to: events.shertoncouncil@gov.uk.

Send an email with your ideas to Sherton Council.

The email should:

→ tell the council your ideas for the festival

→ say why you think these ideas would be popular

→ be approximately 80–120 words long. [6 marks]

[+3 marks for SPaG]

8 **Activity: Write a report**

You recently saw this notice at the train station:

> **Witnesses needed**
>
> Did you see an accident at this station on the morning of 11 October? The accident involved one person with a large wheeled suitcase and another on an electric scooter. It took place near the ticket office.
>
> If you saw the accident, we would be grateful if you could write a report about what you witnessed. Send your report to police.sherton@gov.uk.

In your report, you should:

→ say what the report is about

→ provide information about where you were and when

→ explain what happened

→ conclude by saying who you believe was at fault.

Your report should be between 150 and 250 words long. [20 marks]

9 Your latest dentist appointment was rearranged for an earlier date without informing you. When you did not turn up, you received a text message telling you that you will need to pay a fine for the missed appointment. You rang the receptionist about this, but he was very rude and refused to listen.

Your task: Write a formal letter of complaint to the dentist. The address is: Ms M. Harris, Molars Dental Practice, 1 Pearl Avenue, Newberry, NB1 1BN.

You should include:

- why you are writing
- what the problems were
- why this is unacceptable
- what you would like the dentist to do in response.

You should write about 200–250 words. [27 marks]

10 You see a writing competition in a magazine aimed at young people. They are offering a prize of £150 for the best story about overcoming a difficulty.

Your task: Write a story about a time you had to overcome a difficulty.

You could include:

- how the difficulty began
- what happened next
- how you felt in the worst moment
- how you overcame the difficulty
- how you felt when you had come out on top.

You should write about 250 words. [27 marks]

11 Information

> **Tariq:** It's terrible how much junk food our college canteen serves. Yesterday, the lunch choice was burger and fries, fish and chips, fried chicken or cheese pizza. There's nothing healthy there at all. Junk food should be banned in college canteens. Everyone would benefit from eating better meals with plenty of vegetables.

> **Ashley:** I don't agree at all. Yes, they should add some healthy options like salads, but banning less healthy options? No way! Everyone should have the right to decide for themselves what they eat.

Writing task

Write a contribution to the web forum explaining your views on this topic.

In your contribution, you should:

- say whether unhealthy food should be banned in college canteens
- give detailed reasons for your views.

You should aim to write about 150–200 words. [15 marks]

12 You are the head of a sports club at college. Recently, you have received the following complaints from members:

> The same people are always booking up the badminton courts. It's not fair! We should all take turns so everyone has a chance to use them.

> Some members are leaving dirty clothes and muddy trainers in the changing room. It's beginning to smell horrible in there.

> I found crisp packets floating in the swimming pool today. Crisp packets! Who thinks it's OK to drop litter in a swimming pool?

Write a notice for the club noticeboard. This notice should:
➜ have an introduction, setting out what the problems are
➜ give some helpful rules for people to follow
➜ be easy to read
➜ be approximately 80–120 words long.

[6 marks]

[+3 marks for SPaG]

13 Information

You see the following notice at your community centre:

> I have noticed that fewer people have been using the community centre recently. I want to make sure it is a place everyone can use.
>
> Please write me a report telling me about your experiences at the community centre and any problems you have encountered.
>
> Your report could include sections on:
> - the computer room
> - the community garden
> - the children's play area
> - the café
> - the classes offered. If you attended any dance, fitness, arts and crafts or skills for life classes, I want to know about them.
>
> I would also like you to include recommendations for improvements.
>
> Jacinda Bell
>
> Community Centre Manager

Writing task

Write a report for Jacinda Bell about the community centre.

In your report, you should:
➜ talk about your experience using three things the community centre offers
➜ describe any problems you encountered
➜ suggest improvements that could be made.

You should aim to write about 200–250 words.

[21 marks]

14 Information

> Everyone has a favourite music artist, whether it is a solo singer or a band.
>
> They might play pop music, folk songs or rock ballads.
>
> They might rap or perform R&B.
>
> They might mix amazing dance tunes.
>
> Or they might do something completely different.
>
> Please tell us about two of your favourite music artists and why you think they are special.

Writing task

Write an article for a music website about your favourite music artists.

In your article, you should:

→ say who your favourite music artists are
→ explain why you think they are special.

You should aim to write about 150–200 words. [15 marks]

15 It is your first day working at Space Exploration Labs. You have been asked to write a set of instructions for an alien visiting Earth, telling them how to live as a human for a day.

Your task: Write the instructions.

You should include:

→ how to dress like a human
→ what to do at different times of the day
→ how to greet people and talk to them politely
→ what meals to eat and how often.

You should write about 200–250 words. [27 marks]

Language techniques, layout features and purposes of texts

Language techniques

- Alliteration
- Cliché
- Colloquial language/chatty language
- Direct address
- Emotive language
- Exclamation
- Expert opinions
- Humour
- Hyperbole/exaggeration
- Idiom
- Imagery
- Imperative/command/instruction
- Inclusive language
- Interview/dialogue
- Irony
- Metaphor
- Onomatopoeia
- Oxymoron
- Pathos
- Personification
- Puns/wordplay
- Question and answer
- Quotations
- Repetition
- Rhetorical question
- Rhyme
- Rule of three
- Sarcasm
- Simile
- Statistics

Layout features

- Arrows
- Bold font
- Bullet points
- Capital letters
- Captions
- Chapters
- Charts
- Colour
- Columns
- Diagrams
- Different fonts
- Different sized fonts
- Footnotes
- Highlighting
- Images / pictures
- Italics
- Labels
- Links
- Lists
- Menus
- Paragraphs
- Search boxes/search function
- Sections
- Side bars
- Subheadings
- Symbols
- Tabs
- Text boxes

Purposes of texts

- Advertise
- Advise
- Complain
- Criticise
- Discuss
- Entertain
- Explain
- Inform
- Instruct
- Persuade
- Review
- Summarise / give an overview

Glossary

Adapt: change to fit the current situation.

Adjective: a word that describes an object, person, place or thing (for example, beautiful, red, heavy, clever, exciting).

Answer effectively: answer in a way that gives enough information and fully answers the question.

Appropriate: suitable.

Asterisk: a symbol that looks like this*. It is used to point the reader to more information elsewhere, usually at the bottom of the page.

Audience: the people listening to you (or the people you have written a document for).

Clause: a group of words that contains at least one **verb** or action word (sometimes referred to as a 'doing or being' word) and a **subject** (who or what is doing the action). A clause can form part of a sentence or it can be one whole sentence.

Coherent: organised, logical and consistent. All the different points in your answer should follow on from each other in a way that makes sense.

Compare: find similarities or differences.

Context: the information around something, which you can use to understand its meaning.

Contraction: a shortened version of a word or group of words, made by removing one or more letters. For example: don't (short for *do not*), could've (short for *could have*), and I'm (short for *I am*).

Contribution: a comment or question that adds something to the discussion.

Definite article: the word 'the'.

Dependent clause: a clause that cannot stand on its own as a sentence. A dependent clause will usually explain an independent clause or add extra information to it. It will contain a linking word such as 'because' – this is used to attach the dependent clause to an independent clause.

Descriptive language: words that describe something (tell the reader what something looks, sounds, smells, feels or tastes like).

Evidence: information that backs up arguments and opinions, such as facts, examples, experience, observations and quotes.

Explanatory language: words that explain something to the reader.

Fact: something that can be proved true through observation or science/research. For example, if your friend says 'It is raining outside', you can look out of the window to see if this is true.

Footnote: a small number next to a word, like this[1]. It directs the reader to more information at the bottom of the page.

Formal language: words that are meant for a serious, respectful or important situation. It does not include slang or conversational phrases.

Homophones and near homophones: words that sound the same or similar but that have different meanings, such as: there/their/they're, were/where/we're, to/too/two, are/our.

Identify: find information.

Indefinite article: the word 'a' or 'an'.

Independent clause: a clause that can stand on its own as a sentence.

Infer: work out the meaning of something that is not stated directly.

Informal language: is the opposite of formal language. It is meant for less serious situations, tends to be conversational, and can include slang.

Instructional language: words that tell the reader how to do something.

Interject: add your own contribution to a discussion. Always do this respectfully.

Language: the words you use and how you use them, including to create certain effects.

Language techniques/features: different ways of using words to create a particular effect.

Lines of argument: how the different points that someone makes lead to their opinions or conclusions.

Main points: what the document is about, and its most important ideas and arguments.

Medium: method or type, e.g. the type of speaking you are doing, such as a presentation, a discussion, or a question-and-answer session.

Opinion: a view, belief or judgement. It is not possible to prove that opinions are true or false because they differ from person to person (for example, 'Coffee tastes great').

Organisational and structural features: the ways in which the document has been laid out to help the reader find and understand information.

Paragraph: a section of writing, at least one sentence long but usually several sentences, which is all on one topic or making one point. A new paragraph starts on a new line.

Persuasive language: words that try to make the reader **agree** with a view or **do** something, such as buy a product or come to an event.

Phrases: the words and expressions you use.

Presentation: a prepared speech or talk in which information is given to an audience.

Proper noun: a name or title. For example, people's names, place names, names of companies and organisations, and the titles of books, films and songs.

Punctuation: the use of symbols and spaces in writing to show meaning and help the reader understand.

Purpose: what you are trying to achieve, such as to give information, to explain something or to convince someone.

Reference materials: anything that provides extra information, such as a key (which explains the meaning of different symbols), a caption (which gives extra information about an image), or a glossary (which gives meanings of words).

Registers: the tone of voice you speak with.

Relevant information: what the presentation is about, including the main subjects and any information and facts that relate to these.

Relevant questions: questions that are about the topic being discussed.

Similarities: things that are like each other or that are the same.

Specialist words: words that relate to a specific topic.

Subheadings: below the main title, a heading that begins a new section of the document. Subheadings are normally used to separate different topics and to help the reader quickly see what each section is about.

Subject–verb agreement: the rule that the verb (the action word or 'doing'/'being' word) in a sentence should agree with (match) the subject (what or who is doing the action). In most cases, this is about whether something is plural (more than one) or singular (just one). For example, the verb 'run' needs to change to match the subject, which might be singular (She runs) or plural (They run).

Tenses: a way to express time in your writing by changing how the verb (the action word or the 'doing'/'being' word) is written. For example: He ran, he runs, and he will be running.

Vocabulary: the words the writer has used.

Answers to diagnostic questions

Speaking, listening and communicating

1. **What riding a horse involves, The equipment needed to ride and look after horses, and The presenter's opinion about horse riding.**

   These are the most relevant points to the topic of horse riding. They are the details that would be best to ask questions about. A joke about horses is less important because it is not about horse riding. It was probably intended to keep the presentation interesting for the audience, rather than to give any important information. What the presenter had for breakfast on her first day of horse riding might have been an interesting detail to set the scene, but it is not important to remember. It does not give important information about horse riding, and asking further questions about it will not give more information about horse riding. How long the presenter expects the presentation to take is not about horse riding.

   See 1.1 Identifying relevant information in presentations. See 1.2 Asking relevant questions, as recognising the most important points will help you to ask relevant questions. Also see **1.6 Making contributions in discussions**, as this also requires identifying the most relevant points for further discussion.

2. (c) *What kinds of horses are the best to ride and why?* **and** (d) *How expensive is horse riding as a regular hobby?* **are the best questions to ask.**

   These are the only questions in the list that are about horse riding, so they are the most relevant and useful questions.

   See 1.2 on asking **relevant questions**, and **1.6** on **making contributions in discussions.**

3. *1. Introduce the topic, 2. Present information and ideas, 3. Give your own point of view, 4. Ask if the audience has any questions.*

   This is the best order for giving a presentation that communicates points clearly and effectively. **See 1.4 about communicating clearly** for more advice on giving presentations.

4. **A personal story about your dog providing comfort when you are sad, The fact that a third of all households around the world have a dog, and Explaining the games you can play with a dog and the tricks you can teach it.**

   These pieces of evidence are the most likely to persuade listeners that dogs make great pets. The name of a celebrity's dog might be a fun thing to include, but it is not evidence of why a dog makes a good pet. The fact that dogs evolved from wolves is interesting, but it would not convince someone that a dog is a good pet since wolves are not good pets! Your own opinion cannot be used as evidence to support your own opinion.

   See 1.5 about supporting opinions with evidence, and **1.7 about adapting your comments to suit audience and purpose.**

5. (a) This is an informal situation and the topic is fun and light-hearted. Option (a) reflects this better with light-hearted, chatty

language. Option (b) is too serious. It also does not fully answer the question, as it does not tell us what the presenter thinks is the best holiday. Option (a) does fully answer the question. **See 1.3 about responding to questions effectively.** Also **see 1.7 about adapting your comments to suit audience and purpose.**

(b) This is polite, shows respect for others, and asks a useful question. The fact that you have also climbed the mountain can be used as a positive point, rather than a negative point that puts the speaker down. Option (a) is dismissive and not respectful. It also does not add anything useful or help to find out more information. **See 1.2 about asking relevant questions,** and **1.7 about adapting your comments to suit the audience and the situation.** Also **see 1.8 about respecting others in discussions.**

(b) You should explain any technical words that the audience might find confusing. You do not need to avoid technical words altogether, as using some might be necessary when explaining your topic. **See 1.4 about communicating clearly,** and **1.7 about using words and phrases that are suitable for the situation.**

Reading

1 This question is all about language techniques. **See 2.4 for more information on language techniques.**

Exaggeration ➜ This is the most exciting thing that's ever happened! Exaggeration, also knows as hyperbole, is the technique of using over-the-top statements that are not meant to be taken literally. When someone says that something is the most exciting thing that's ever happened, this is very unlikely to be literally true! Instead, they are exaggerating how exciting it is. Recognising when someone is exaggerating will also help you to understand meaning in texts, as well as recognise opinions. **See 2.3 on meaning, and on facts and opinions.**

Rule of three ➜ We offer cycling, horse-riding and lakeside walks. Rule of three is the technique of presenting things in 3s so that we take more notice, and so it sticks in our mind better. This statement is an example of rule of three because there are 3 activities mentioned – cycling, horse-riding, lakeside walks. Did you pick 'Sale at Tiny Tony's toyshop today'? That is not rule of three because there are 4 Ts – 2 big Ts and 2 small ts. Nothing is presented in a 3.

Direct address ➜ You will not regret it. Direct address is when the author talks straight to the reader. Usually, they will do this by using the word 'you'. Another way to speak directly to the reader is to give them a command or instruction. For example: 'Put the sugar into a large bowl.' 'Do it now!'

Alliteration ➜ Sale at Tiny Tony's toyshop today! Alliteration is the technique of using the same letters at the beginning of related words. The words don't have to be all in a row, although in this case they are: Tiny Tony's toyshop today – four Ts!

2 This question is all about purpose and the vocabulary used to achieve that purpose. For more **about purpose and vocabulary, see 2.8.** Also **see 2.4 for more about language.**

To make people buy a product → Persuasive language. Persuasive language is used to make someone do something or make someone agree with a view. Advertisements tend to include a lot of persuasive language because they want to convince the reader to buy something.

To tell people how to make a meal → Instructional language. Instructions are used to tell someone how to do something.

To help people understand something → Explanatory language. Explanatory language is used to explain things.

To complain about something → Critical or negative language. Critical language can mean that something includes a lot of negative comments or comments that judge something badly. Alternatively, critical language can sometimes just mean including judgements, either good or bad. In either case, critical language is often used when reviewing something or when complaining about something.

3   This question is all about using punctuation to understand meaning in texts. **See 2.10 for more about understanding punctuation and its uses.**

Katie has more than one sister → True. The apostrophe after the s on the word sisters tells us that the advice belongs to more than one sister.

In the second sentence, commas have been used to separate items in a list → True. The items are: smart trousers, a buttoned shirt, a black jacket and black shoes. The commas separate them so that we know where each item ends, and so we don't have to keep repeating the word 'and'.

The apostrophe in the third sentence indicates belonging → False. The apostrophe appears in the word didn't. It is actually telling us that this is a contraction (of 'did not') and so there is a letter missing in this word.

The full name of the department store is Dimble's → False. The capital letters tell us that the full name is Dimble's Great Department Store. A great department store just called Dimble's would be written like this: 'Dimble's, the great department store.'

The exclamation mark at the end tells us this is a command → False. This exclamation mark is emphasising Katie's success, and perhaps conveying a sense of excitement too. The last sentence is definitely not a command.

4   This question is all about understanding the difference between facts and opinions. **See 2.3 for more about facts and opinions.**

It is hard to stay indoors when the sun is shining → Opinion. Whether it is hard to stay indoors or not is an opinion that will differ from person to person. One person might find it hard, but another might not.

Staying in the shade is a good idea on a hot day → Opinion. One person might think this is a good idea. They might have a lot of good reasons for thinking this, and you might agree with them, but not everyone will agree! It differs from person to person.

Tickets for the festival cost £50 per person → Fact. This can be proved true or false. It does not differ from person to person.

Affordable tickets are available from the council → Opinion. This is a tricky one, because it might seem like a fact at first. We can prove whether tickets are available from the council or not. However, the word 'affordable' turns this into an opinion. One person's idea of what is affordable might be very different from another person's idea of what is affordable. It differs from person to person, and so it must be an opinion.

5. This question is about finding the main points of documents. **See 2.1 for more about main points and details in documents.**

   The correct answer is **(b) *The subheadings.*** In most cases, the subheadings will tell you the main points of a document because they sum up the information in the paragraphs below them. **See 2.6 for more information about organisational features.**

   (a) *The image captions* is not correct because the caption usually just gives more information about the image. **See 2.6 for more about organisational features,** and **2.5 for more about using reference materials.**

   (c) *The footnotes* is not correct because the footnotes usually give information about a specific word or specific point in the document. **See 2.6 for more about organisational features,** and also **2.5 for more about using reference materials.**

   (d) *The tabs and links* is not correct because tabs usually send you to the main parts of a website, rather than tell you the main points of a document. Links usually send you to another place to find out more information or to complete a task. **See 2.6 for more about organisational features.**

6. This question is about understanding the meaning of images. **See 2.7 for more about questions on images.**

   The correct answer is **(d) *No drinks allowed inside.*** The sign shows a drink with a line through it. This is a common sign used in shops and public places to show that drinks are not allowed. If you find it hard to see this meaning in the image, remember that you can also find the right answer by getting rid of the wrong answers.

   (a) *Sold out of drinks* is not correct because we have been told the shop sells clothes. It would make no sense for a clothes shop to put up a sign that means 'sold out of drinks'. **See 2.3 for more about understanding meaning by looking at context.**

   (b) *Shop closed at lunchtime* is not correct because there is nothing in the image to suggest lunchtime. People have drinks at any time of the day. If the sign showed food or a meal, this option might be more likely to be true, but all it shows is a drink.

   (c) *This cannot be recycled* is not correct for two reasons. The first reason is that the image does not show something being recycled or thrown away. The second reason is that this sign appears outside a clothes shop, not on something people might try to recycle such as packaging. **See 2.3 for more about understanding meaning by looking at context.**

7. Firstly, did you notice this instruction before question 7: *You will need to use the source documents on pages 58-60 to answer the next questions?*

   If you did not read this properly, you were probably very confused by the rest of the questions in this section. It is easy to miss instructions when you are trying to get through an exam paper quickly. Try not to do this! It is very important to pay attention to everything in the question paper, including instructions like this. See the **Assessment Breakdown** section on page 7 to 8 to find out more about what to expect on each part of your exam.

Answers to diagnostic questions 105

OK, let's get back to question 7!

This question is about finding one specific detail in the text. For more about **details and main points in texts, see 2.1.**

The correct answer is **(c) Happy Travels Magazine.** You can find it at the bottom of Document 1. The names of magazines are often included at the top or bottom of each page in a magazine. It is a good place to start when looking for a name.

(a) *Document 1: Magazine* is not the correct answer because this is telling us the document number and the type of text it is. If you look at each source document, you can see that they all have this label at the top, explaining which number document it is and what text type it is. It is therefore not the magazine's name.

(b) *Four holiday ideas you should consider* is not the correct answer because this is the title of the article in the magazine, not the magazine's name. **See 2.6 on organisational features.**

(d) *Packing essentials* is not the correct answer because this is the subheading of one section in the document, not the magazine's name. **See 2.6 on organisational features.**

8 This question is about using reference materials to find information. **See 2.5 on using reference materials.**

The correct answer is **(a) Coastal Cruiser.** Finding this answer is a two-step process. Start by looking for the most popular holidays in Document 2. They are shown under the subheading 'Our most popular holidays'. None of these holidays mention breakfasts and dinners, so we need to find more information. Below this section there is a box that explains the meanings of three different symbols. The third symbol says 'Breakfasts and dinners included.' So that means the holidays marked with that symbol do include breakfasts and dinners. We need to answer with the holiday that does not include breakfasts and dinners, so we need to find which holiday does not have this symbol. The only one that does not is Coastal Cruiser – so that must be our answer!

Neither (b) *Cornwall and Cream Teas*, nor (c) *Scottish Supertour* can be correct because they both have the symbol that means breakfasts and dinners are included. If you answered with one of these, you did manage to complete the first step in the two-step process – you found the most popular holidays! But you needed to keep going to find more information. As these questions often involve looking in places such as boxes, labels, keys, diagrams, etc, it would be useful to look at **2.6 on organisational features as well as 2.5 on using reference materials.**

(d) *Mainline Miracle Tours* is not the correct answer because this is the name of the company that offers the holidays, not the name of one of its most popular holidays. **See 2.1 on looking for details in texts and 2.6 on organisational features.** You need to be prepared to look anywhere in the source document for answers, not just in the main text.

9 This question is about using a dictionary to find meanings of words, and about fitting a word into its context. **See 2.5 for more about dictionary questions. See 2.9 for more about understanding specialist words in context. Also see 2.3 for more about meaning and context.**

The correct answer is **b Modernise.** First, look up the meaning of 'renovate'. Renovate does not mean to sell or to scrap something, so neither (a) nor (c) can be the correct answer. We can rule those out. So what about (d)? The dictionary will tell us that renovating something can involve restoring it, so this seems like the correct answer. But wait! We need to replace the word renovate while keeping the meaning of the sentence the same. Let's try it. *It is vital that we restoration all caravans older than eight years.* That doesn't work! We would need the word to be 'restore' but it isn't, so we can rule out 'restoration' as well. That means we're left with 'modernise'. This does fit into the sentence! Does it fit the definition of 'renovate'? Yes, because renovating something can mean modernising it. So, 'modernise' is the answer.

10   This question is about comparing source documents. **See 2.2 for more on comparison questions. Also see 2.1 on finding main points and details in texts.**

You can visit attractions → Similar. Both documents say this. Document 1: 'visits to all sorts of attractions'. Document 2: 'visit top attractions'.

You will only travel on trains → Different. Look at the bottom of Document 2: 'Some bus travel to attractions will be necessary.' If you travel on a bus, you are not travelling by train alone. **See 2.6 on organisational features,** as finding this answer involves looking beyond the main text (in this case, in the boxes).

You will not do any physical activity → Different. Look at the last bullet point in Document 2: 'a good level of physical fitness is essential for walking tours, climbing steps, hikes and carrying luggage between trains.' That's a long list of different kinds of physical activity that these holidays involve. **See 2.3 on understanding meaning in texts.**

All your meals will be included → Different. Look at the second bullet point in Document 2: 'Some meals provided on select holidays.' Only some meals are provided, and only on some (select) holidays. This means that not all meals are included. **See 2.3 on understanding meaning in texts.**

Writing

1   This question is about using commas correctly. **See 3.1 on punctuation. Also see 3.7 on commas in complex sentences.** The correct placement of the commas is shown in brackets below:

Because we've run out of a few essentials(,) I need you to pick up some things from the shops. Please buy bread(,) milk and cheese. As a way of saying thank you(,) I will make you a lovely dinner. Thanks!

2   This question is about punctuation. **See 3.1 for more information on different kinds of punctuation.** The correct placement of the missing punctuation is shown in brackets below:

What is your favourite meal(?) Mine is pizza and my sister Emily(')s is pasta, but our brothers love curries. I asked them why(.) They explained that they prefer spicy food.

3   This question is about correct grammar. The correct words are in bold below:

*Playing board games **is** a great way to spend time with family. You can even use games to teach **a** child to read, count and think ahead. **They're** a lot of fun!*

Answers to diagnostic questions   107

is – Read about **subject–verb agreement in 3.2 grammar.**

a – Read about **definite and indefinite articles in 3.2 grammar.**

They're – Read about **homophones in 3.2 grammar.**

4 This question is about correct word order in sentences. **See 3.2 on grammar and also 3.7 on constructing sentences.** The correct sentences are:

The train arrived earlier than expected.

I didn't have time to eat breakfast.

What do you like doing at the weekend?

5 This question is about common spelling mistakes. **See 3.3 on spelling.** The correct spellings are:

because, definitely, writing, sincerely

6 This question is about writing with an appropriate level of detail. **See 3.5 on detail.**

The correct answers are **(b) The type and amount of litter in the lunch area,** and **(e) Who you have seen making a mess in the lunch area.**

These are the most important details to include because they are most relevant to the task (complaining about the unclean and untidy state of the lunch area). The principal needs to know what the problem is if you want them to fix it. **See 3.4 on writing accurate answers.** Knowing who is making the mess will also help the principal to solve the problem, so this is more useful than the other options.

7 This question is about writing in a logical order and structuring your answer using paragraphs. **See 3.4 on writing clearly and coherently, 3.6 on structure, and 3.7 on writing in paragraphs.**

First paragraph ➜ You are going to suggest different holiday ideas. It is important to first tell your friend why you are writing.

Second paragraph ➜ Your first choice would be to go skiing. It makes sense to mention your first choice before other choices.

Third paragraph ➜ A trip to a warm, sandy beach would be lovely. More choices or information should be given before concluding the email.

Final paragraph ➜ You would like your friend to reply to your email. The final paragraph should tell your friend how you would like them to respond.

8 This question is about using format, structure and language that is suitable for purpose and audience. **See 3.6 on format, structure and language.**

Writing task	Type of language	Essential structures
Write an exciting story about a day when something amazing happened.	Entertaining	Story structure: • Beginning, middle and end, usually told in the order things happened.
Write a letter to the council to complain about problems in your area.	Critical	Letter structure: • Addresses • Date • Opening salutation • Appropriate close

Writing task	Type of language	Essential structures
Write a notice to tell people how to recycle properly.	Instructional	**Notice structure:** **A title is needed for a notice. In addition, instructions should be separated using one of more of the following:** - **Numbers** - **Bullet points** - **Paragraphs** - **Sections** - **Subheadings**

Answers to diagnostic questions

Index

adjectives 41
advertisement writing 86–7
apostrophes 56, 68–9
article writing 84
asterisks 43
audience, adapting to 23–4, 81
body language 25
brackets 56
bullet points 45
capital letters 67–9
clauses 67, 69, 90–1
commas 56, 67–9, 90–1
comparisons 35–6
complaining 79–80
complex sentences 67, 89–91
composition 76–8
compound sentences 90–1
context 38–9, 54–5
contractions 68–9
definite article 71–2
dependent clause 90–1
descriptive language 52
diary entries 84
dictionary use 8–9, 43, 54
discussion *see* group discussion; question and answer session
emails 72, 77, 83
evidence 20
exam countdown 6
exclamation marks 56, 68–9
explanatory language 52
facts 38–40
feedback forms 85
footnotes 43
formal language 52
forum contributions 85
full stops 67–9
grammar 71–2
group discussion 14, 21–6
   exam 7
homophones 71–2, 74
images 48–9
indefinite article 71–2
independent clause 90–1
inference 48–9
informal language 52
information sheets 85
instructional language 52
joining words 90–1

language
   appropriate 25, 81
   techniques 41–2
   types of 52, 81
layout features 45–6
letter writing 69, 74–5, 82
lines of argument 12
linking words 90–1
listening 12, 25
main points 33
meanings 38, 48–9
medium 23
narratives 71, 84
newsletters 84
nouns 67
open questions 14
opinion 38–40
organisational features 45–6
paragraphs 45, 89
persuasive language 52
phrases 23, 41
plurals 71
presentation 12
   adapting 23
   evidence 20
   exam 7
   listening 12
   preparation 17–18
   question and answer session 12–16, 25
   source document 27
   structure 17–19
proper nouns 67
punctuation 56–7, 67–9
purpose 51, 81
question and answer session 12–16, 25
   see also group discussion
question marks 68–9
questions, open 14
reading
   comparisons 35–6
   context 38–9
   exam 7–8
   inference 48–9
   main points 33
   meanings 38, 48–9
   organisational features 45–6
   punctuation 56–7

reference materials 43
   source document 58–60
   specialist words 54–5
   subheadings 33, 45–6
   textual devices 41–2
   vocabulary 51–5
reference materials 43
   see also dictionary use
registers 23
relevant information 12
report writing 83
respect 25
review writing 84
sentences 67, 89–91
similarities 35
simple sentences 90
specialist words 54–5, 74
speech marks 68
spelling 74–5
structural features 45–6
subheadings 33, 45–6
subject-verb agreement 71–2
tenses 71–2
textual devices 41–2
tone of voice 23
vocabulary 51–5
witness statements 85
writing
   advertisements 86–7
   articles 84
   capital letters 67
   composition 76–8
   diary entries 84
   emails 72, 77, 83
   exam 9
   feedback forms 85
   grammar 71–2
   information sheets 85
   instructions 86
   language choice 81
   letters 69, 74–5, 82
   narratives 71, 84
   newsletters 84
   paragraphs 45, 89
   punctuation 56–7, 67–9
   reports 83
   reviews 84
   specialist words 74
   spelling 74–5